God without the Idea of Evil

God without the Idea of Evil

JEAN-MIGUEL GARRIGUES, O.P.

Translated by Gregory Casprini, O.S.B.

Foreword by Christoph Cardinal Schönborn, O.P.

University of Notre Dame Press

Notre Dame, Indiana

Copyright © 2023 by the University of Notre Dame
Notre Dame, Indiana 46556
undpress.nd.edu

All Rights Reserved

Original French version ©2016, Éditions Ad Solem

Published in the United States of America

Library of Congress Control Number: 2023937451

ISBN: 978-0-268-20541-6 (Hardback)
ISBN: 978-0-268-20543-0 (WebPDF)
ISBN: (978-0-268-20540-9 (Epub)

*To my brothers and sisters in Saint Dominic,
Saint Thomas Aquinas, and Saint Catherine of Sienna,
with whom God has enabled me to discover the
"interior chamber or cell" as the mercy of his Fatherly heart,
in which nothing has been able to separate us*

Are you not from of old,
    O Lord my God, my Holy One?
    You shall not die.
Your eyes are too pure to behold evil,
    and you cannot look on wrongdoing;
why do you look on the treacherous,
    and are silent when the wicked swallow
    those more righteous than they?

—Habakkuk 1:12–13

Now the men who were holding Jesus
began to mock him and beat him;
they also blindfolded him and kept asking him,
"Prophesy! Who is it that struck you?"

—Luke 22:63–64

CONTENTS

Foreword ix
by Cardinal Christoph Schönborn, O.P.

Translator's Preface xiii

Introduction xxi

PART ONE.
THE MYSTERY

ONE. The Omnipotence of the Father   3

TWO. The Humanity of God   26

THREE. The Innocence of the Father in Our Adoption   42

FOUR. The Glorious Growth of the Liberty of the Sons of God   55

FIVE. The Goodwill "Even unto Madness"
of the Lamb of God   67

SIX. The Vulnerability of God as the Lamb   78

PART TWO.
THE ECONOMY OF THE MYSTERY

SEVEN. The Son as the Lamb Who Was Slain from the Beginning of the World   93

EIGHT. Gethsemane: The Supreme Contradiction of Evil   102

NINE. The Mysterious Ambivalence of the Cup   119

TEN. In the Cell of Mercy   132

PART THREE.
AN UNDERSTANDING OF THE MYSTERY

ELEVEN. God without the Idea of Evil   147

TWELVE. How Does God Know the Evil of Which He Has No Idea?   164

Notes   171

Index   177

FOREWORD

In this book, two images serve as the iconographic basis for a certain number of far-reaching theological considerations: the Blessed Fra Angelico's fresco of the *Mocking of Christ* and Saint Andrei Rublev's icon of the Trinity. The symbolic value of these two images expresses the full weight of the mystery contemplated throughout these pages: the mystery of God's innocence. Fr. Jean-Miguel Garrigues is well aware of the fact that he is treating here an extremely controversial issue. How is God to be situated in the face of evil? In the past there were numerous attempts to elaborate a type of theodicy that seeks, with greater or lesser success, to rationally and philosophically "excuse" God for the presence of evil in the world, for evil that seems to contradict the goodness of God. In our own day there is a trend toward an opposite kind of "theodicy," one that attempts to justify God in the face of evil by attributing to him the suffering that derives from the possibility, or from the actual fact, of being subject to evil and sin.

Father Garrigues has had the courage to approach this problem in a new way, with rigorous precision and a desire for objectivity. This is something that merits particular appreciation, because there has been a general tendency to consider this subject only through the prism of our sensitivity, which is not completely purified. The author attempts to clearly illustrate all that the light of faith brings to this problem, and he seeks in this way to transmit to us the joy that is infallibly inspired by the truth.

Fra Angelico depicts Christ as being mocked while his eyes are covered by a veil. In this way, he is presented as the icon of God who, according to the expression of Saint Thomas Aquinas, "has no idea of evil." In fact, according to the explanation of Father Garrigues, God in no way foresees or plans for moral evil. He does not even "see it" in the proper sense of the term, because he does not conceive it. From an ontological point of view, he is infinitely removed from voluntary evil and has nothing in common with it. Is this an exaggeration? A timorous desire to "save" God from the tempest of the problem of evil? Step by step, our author leads us to discover a new meaning to the above-mentioned expression of Saint Thomas.

God without the idea of evil: in the first part of the book, we are made to consider the "innocent benevolence of the creative design of the Father." Indeed, in this design, God the Father sees man exclusively insomuch as he has called him to be his heir, his adopted son. "Creation itself is only the first act of a design of adoption," which is the goal of creation, its "orientation." If this is "the orientation of creation, which gives it its proper form," then the liberty of the spiritual creature occupies a central place in God's plan. Starting with creation, we are called by grace to respond voluntarily, freely, to the divine love that confers on us the gift of being by bringing us into existence.

The pages in which Father Garrigues contemplates the mystery of our election are admirable; this mystery is expressed in the very fact of our existence. "God elects us precisely by creating us from nothing." By enveloping us in his look, "God encounters us in the very gift of being that he bestows upon us, and his eyes do not see our sin." God's gaze always encompasses us in the freshness of his creative act, which is the origin of our existence. Father Garrigues invites us to rediscover in the eyes of Jesus, the eternal charm, the continually new charm of the divine look that chooses us by calling us into existence. God does not see the evil in us! Indeed, "his eyes are too pure to behold evil" (Hab. 1:13).

But if this is so, what then is evil? It is merely "the falsification of our true good," a "deprivation of being, which is only possible in created beings, for whom being is something which they 'have,' and which they may partly lose." Moral evil is a part of the good that is the object of man's desire but that he isolates and sets up as an absolute, in place of the divine good.

If God continually gazes upon us in his creative look, how does he deal with evil? In the second part of the book, Father Garrigues contemplates how God's design in creating the world, in adopting man, and in bringing him into communion with himself, goes through "the contradictions of evil." A synthesis of these considerations is found in Rublev's icon: on the table, placed amid the three visiting angels, we can see a cup. Basing himself on an intuition of Saint Catherine of Siena, Father Garrigues examines the significance of this cup: he sees in it the symbol of the freedom of man. It thus signifies the only possible way in which we can receive the blood that has been shed by God out of love. It is indeed the "cup of blessing," but it can turn into a cup of wrath, if the freedom of man, who is invited to consent and accept, puts up instead a resolute refusal. The finest pages of this very rich book are perhaps those dealing with the garden of Gethsemane. The author here quotes Saint Catherine of Siena, who sees in the cup of the agony of Christ not so much the fear of physical suffering but rather the "suffering of desire," the ultimate test of the vulnerability of divine love in the face of evil: this suffering derives from the possibility that "God's thirst for our salvation" can be frustrated by us and that "the '*no*' of man's resolute refusal, can ultimately thwart the divine purpose."

A God overcome by evil? The Lord's divine work destroyed by the refusal of his own creature? Absolutely not! The "redemptive charity of Christ in his agony will continue to love without taking into account that a refusal is always possible. Instead the Lord will move forward, with eyes veiled against the contradiction of evil." He will love despite the refusal, drawing this love from his creative charity. That is why he "does not accept evil but permits the freedom that can cause evil. . . . God does not permit evil; he only permits the liberty that can commit the evil act." Father Garrigues confronts us with the ultimate possibility of sin: the last and final refusal of love, the "self-punishment" of damnation when "the torrent of God's love flows into persons who use their liberty to destroy it" and who are therefore compared by our author to the "black holes" of the cosmos. "These people, who have become focused forever uniquely upon themselves, are able to suffocate the divine love that is within them, just as all light is extinguished in the 'black holes' of outer space, holes that have become incapable of reflecting or radiating any energy whatsoever."

Father Garrigues's book has sparked considerable debate among certain experts on Saint Thomas Aquinas. This is why, starting with the second edition, the author decided to add a third part, which, in a more technical manner, elucidates the controversy surrounding the book. In this section, Father Garrigues defines in a precise manner the terms he has employed, continuing theological reflection along lines that were traced out by Jacques Maritain and Cardinal Journet, who devoted more extensive studies to this subject. We invite readers interested in this kind of theological controversy to begin with part 3. That will make it easier to enter more fully into the considerations that constitute the essential theme of the entire book.

God without the Idea of Evil is a meditation of both great theological importance and deep contemplative value. The book has its place among the best works of Dominican spirituality.

Christoph Cardinal Schönborn, O.P.
Archbishop of Vienna

TRANSLATOR'S PREFACE

In a lengthy and colorful autobiographical interview, the title of which could perhaps be best translated as "Sticking to the *Straight and Narrow*: The Itinerary of a Religious Friar in Uncertain Times,"[1] Jean-Miguel Garrigues describes the various stages of his life. The interview reveals someone who is a keen observer of people and events, a man of exceptional human and spiritual caliber. Born into a family of Spanish diplomats in 1944 while his parents were stationed in Istanbul, Turkey, raised and educated in Spain, Italy, and France, Garrigues suddenly decided to join the order of Saint Dominic in France after studying diplomacy for one year at Georgetown University in Washington, DC. His novitiate and priestly formation took place in the mid-1960s, at a time when the French Dominicans, absorbing the initial shocks caused by the post–Vatican II crisis as well as the political and cultural revolution of May 1968, seemed to be radically questioning many of their long-accepted traditional values and truths. It was a chaotic period during which many brothers lost their vocations and even their faith.

Brother Jean-Miguel, however, persevered, and thanks to contact with the older generation of Dominican professors, as well as with seasoned theologians like Jacques Maritain and Louis Bouyer, he succeeded in acquiring a theological formation solidly grounded in the church fathers, Saint Thomas Aquinas, and the magisterium but which also allowed him to remain open to respectful, convivial dialogues on the ecumenical, intellectual, and cultural levels with people from many other horizons.

Garrigues was ordained a priest in 1969 and was granted a scholarship from the World Council of Churches. This enabled him to spend the first year of preparation for his PhD at the Orthodox Faculty of Theology of Thessaloniki (Greece) and the second year at the Faculty of Theology of the Institut Catholique in Paris (ICP). In 1973 he defended his dissertation, titled "Divinisation through Charity according to Maximus the Confessor."

In 1975 Father Garrigues left the Dominicans, temporarily as it turned out, in order to help create a new fraternity of apostolic monks (*les moines apostoliques*). This gave him the opportunity over a period of more than twenty years to share with other brothers in a simple community life and to revitalize together parishes, successively, in three cities of southern France: Aix-en-Provence, Avignon, and Lyons. Each day the community celebrated not only the holy Eucharist but also the entire liturgy of the hours with the active participation of the parishioners. The brothers took turns doing the cooking and accomplishing all the other household chores. During this period Garrigues served as chaplain in a cancer clinic, an experience that later inspired him to write a book about death and eternal life; its title in English could be rendered as *Receiving Eternal Life at the Hour of Our Death*.[2] Elsewhere, Garrigues exercised an intensive pastoral ministry, making himself available in particular to those who had suffered in their lives or who tended to feel marginalized with regard to the church.

Alongside all these activities, Garrigues rapidly earned for himself an excellent reputation as a scholar, theologian, and spiritual writer. He is the author of twenty books on theology and spirituality, as well as numerous articles. In 1981 he published, with a preface by Louis Bouyer, a book on the filioque (the procession of the Holy Spirit in the Trinity),[3] which was an important contribution to the ongoing dialogue between the Catholic and Orthodox Churches.

God without the Idea of Evil (*Dieu sans idée tu mal*) is by far Jean-Miguel Garrigues's most popular work.[4] First published in 1982, it already contains many of the author's deepest and most original theological intuitions concerning God's merciful design of salvation, human liberty, and the problem of evil. Garrigues would develop these themes further in his later writings. The first edition of the book was rapidly translated into Spanish and Polish. An expanded edition appeared in 1990, and this was reedited in 2016 with a preface by Cardinal Christoph Schönborn. In his preface Schönborn states that the work "is a meditation both of great theological importance and deep contemplative value" and that "it has its place among the best works of Dominican spirituality." (It is this 2016 edition that serves as the basis for the present translation.)

Schönborn and Garrigues first became acquainted as young friars when they sat in class together at the Saulchoir, the Dominican school of studies near Paris, during the early days of their theological formation. Their viewpoints on a great number of important questions concerning the church and the world coincided from the beginning, and this gave rise to a lifelong working friendship between them. As soon as he was appointed secretary of Cardinal Joseph Ratzinger's committee for the drafting of the new universal catechism decreed by John Paul II, Schönborn requested the help of his former classmate as well as that of other theological experts. And thus over a period of two years, from 1991 to 1992, Jean-Miguel Garrigues played a significant role alongside Schönborn in the preparation of the *Catechism of the Catholic Church*. The process began with the composition of an initial document following the orientations given by Ratzinger and the bishops of the committee. This preliminary text was then sent to the bishops and pontifical theology faculties all over the world. These, in turn, sent back proposed amendments that had to be evaluated and that, along with those received from Cardinal Ratzinger and the Holy Father himself, had to be integrated into the text the following year.

After Schönborn became cardinal archbishop of Vienna, he and Garrigues were appointed together as the official representatives of the church in a dialogue with Jewish groups who recognize Jesus as the Messiah and who are interested in exploring the continuity between the traditions of Judaism and the liturgy and rituals of the Catholic Church. The encounters took place regularly over a period of sixteen years, in Jerusalem or in Rome. Subsequently, Mark Kinzer, a leading Messianic theologian, invited Garrigues to attend several theological symposiums in the United States on Christian and Messianic theology. In connection with this, Garrigues published an article, "The Jewishness of the Apostles and Its Implications for the Apostolic Church," in the English edition of *Nova et Vetera* (2014). One of his current projects is the preparation of a work in which he plans to show, against the theory of "supersessionism," that the church of the Gentiles did not purely and simply replace the people of Israel.

Prior to his encounters with Kinzer, Garrigues had directed and contributed to a collected work titled *The One and Only Israel of God: Ways for Christians to Approach the Mystery of Israel* (1987).[5] This book soon caught the attention of one of France's best-known sons of Israel, Jean-Marie Lustiger, cardinal archbishop of Paris, whose mother had perished at Auschwitz and who always considered his own baptism into the Catholic Church at age fourteen as not a "conversion" but rather a logical consequence of his Judaism, in perfect continuity with his faith in the God of his ancestors. Cardinal Lustiger invited Garrigues to fill the prestigious role of "Lenten preacher" at the Cathedral of Notre-Dame in Paris for a three-year cycle, from 1993 to 1996. The overall theme chosen for the conferences was the design of God and its realization in salvation history through the successive covenants revealed in the Bible. The program was conceived as a vast catechesis, or series of religious instructions for adults, in the spirit of the church fathers. The first year was devoted to the Old Testament, in which the covenants with Adam, Noah, Abraham, and Moses are established. The second was centered on the unique mediator between God and men, Jesus Christ, in whom the covenants of the Old Testament, far from being abolished, find their fulfillment. The third year was consecrated to the church, the sacrament of salvation, in which all these covenants are disseminated among men until their final accomplishment in glory. In accordance with Lustiger's wishes, Garrigues sought to show how the various biblical covenants of God with humanity are sources of light enabling us to better understand the great cultural, ethical, social, and political questions of our day. The substance of these conferences was later published by Garrigues in a book whose title could be translated as *The Design of God as Seen through His Covenants: Religious Instruction for Adults*.[6]

Lustiger also invited Garrigues to teach at the new seminary he had created, the Paris-Notre-Dame Theology Faculty, and he appointed him to be his special adviser on Catholic theology in its relation to the Jewish people. In 1995 the cardinal requested that Garrigues accompany him on a trip to Israel to attend a seminar on the Shoah at the University of Tel Aviv. As Garrigues recalls, it was a highly dramatic visit during which Lustiger himself received a great deal of unexpected media attention and, initially, a certain amount of hostility from at least one Orthodox Jewish leader, disconcerted by this high-ranking member of the Catholic hierarchy who claimed that in becoming a Christian he still remained faithful to his Jewish heritage. Lustiger's humility, however, quickly won over Israeli public opinion, and his concluding address at the University of Tel Aviv seminar — in which, "without explicitly mentioning either Jesus Christ or the Christian faith, he declared that the vocation of the Jew is to be, by the singularity of his election, the servant of universality among the nations" — was received with fervent enthusiasm. At this same seminar Garrigues also gave a conference titled "The Christian Religious Conscience and the Shoah."[7]

Not long afterward, the future cardinal Georges Cottier, O.P., who was at that time the official theologian of John Paul II, asked Garrigues to deliver the conclusive theological lectures at two Vatican symposiums ("Christian Roots of Anti-Semitism" in 1997 and on the Inquisition in 1998).[8] These lectures were intended to prepare the acts of repentance of John Paul II during the Great Jubilee of the year 2000.

In his conference at the Vatican against anti-Judaism, Garrigues, starting from *Nostra aetate* of Vatican II and continuing with the teaching of John Paul II and the *Catechism of the Catholic Church*, passed in review the various stages of what he calls a "rectification" or "correcting" of false theological opinions that were once widely prevalent in Christendom and that inculcated disdain against the Jewish people. These erroneous ideas, which contradict the authentic place of the children of Israel in the plan of salvation as it is revealed in the New Testament, sometimes served as a pretext for those who sought, supposedly in the name of Christ and the church, to discriminate against and persecute the Jews, forcing them to convert to Christianity, expelling them, or even massacring them. It was necessarily incumbent on the church, declared Garrigues and echoing John Paul II, "to make reparation by an act of penance for the blindness in this domain of some of her children and even a certain number of her ministers." Going further, he added that "without excluding the possibility that, thanks to the universal proclamation of the Gospel by the Church, some sons of Israel adhere freely to Christ, illuminated by inner grace (2 Cor. 3:14–16), Catholics must reject as an action which is in the proper sense contrary to the faith, any type of proselytism that would seek to abolish by human means the presence of Israel in history." Instead,

"Christians must accept the fact that companionship with the Jewish people is a part of the *mystery* (Rom. 11:25) of the plan of salvation during the entire time of the Church."

Around 1995, the community of apostolic monks at the parish of Saint Nizier in Lyons where Father Garrigues had been working for thirteen years came to the sad realization that it would no longer be able continue its mission. The brothers had been living happily together, and their ministry at the parish was greatly appreciated, but most were advancing in age and there was no longer any prospect of attracting younger vocations. After a time of hesitation and searching, Garrigues asked to return to the Dominicans, the order where he first made profession. Since then he has been living and working in the Dominican province of Toulouse, teaching patristic and dogmatic theology at the Thomas Aquinas Institute, leading numerous spiritual retreats, acting as a corresponding member of the Pontifical Academy of Theology in Rome, and continuing to publish various books and articles relating to theology, spirituality, and the life of the church.

In 2015, between the two extraordinary Synods of Bishops on the Family, Garrigues was interviewed by Antonio Spadaro, S.J., editor of *La Civiltà Cattolica*.[9] The article, which is said to have favorably impressed the Holy Father, was translated into English and published in the June 2015 issue of *America* magazine under the title, "A Church of the Pure or a Mixed Fish Net? An Interview with Jean-Miguel Garrigues, O.P."[10] After the second synod on the family, Garrigues published his most recent book in collaboration with a Jesuit theologian, Alain Thomasset, defending and explaining the authentic teaching of Pope Francis given in the apostolic exhortation *Amoris laetitia*. The title of the book could be rendered as *A Morality That Is Flexible but Not without a Compass: A Response to the Doubts Expressed by Certain Cardinals concerning "Amoris laetitia."*[11]

It remains to say a word about how this translation of Garrigues's *God without the Idea of Evil* came into existence. For me it represents the culmination of a journey that began more than forty years ago. Having been born and raised in New York, my native language is English. At age twenty-three, after my conversion and baptism, I entered the Benedictine Abbey of Solesmes in France and lived there for twenty-five years. In 1998 I was sent by Solesmes with other brothers to found a new monastery in Lithuania. I first read *Dieu sans idée du mal* shortly after its publication in 1982. At the time I was studying for the priesthood at Solesmes, and the book, with its poetic meditations on scripture, illustrated by two beautiful icons, helped me not only to grapple inwardly with the difficult problems relating to the existence of evil, human liberty, and God's grace but also and above all to discover how theology can become a beautiful road to contemplation and prayer. It was twenty-five years later, in Lithuania, that I came across the second edition of Garrigues's book, with its supplementary explanations showing how the principal theme of the meditations in part 1, concerning the absolute innocence of God with regard to moral evil, is firmly grounded in the speculative theology of Saint Thomas. After an intensive study of the book, I was able to use it as the basis of a retreat given to religious communities of sisters in French, English, and Lithuanian.

In the meantime, I sent an email to Father Garrigues, whom I had never met, and was amazed to receive an immediate and very friendly reply. On my invitation he came to give conferences at our monastery in Lithuania. He, in turn, encouraged me to take part each year in his summer theology sessions in the south of France. I soon translated several of his articles or conferences destined for an American public, and little by little the idea of translating *Dieu sans idée du mal* was born.

According to the old Latin adage, *Omnis traductor, traditor* (Every translator is a traitor). This translation, however, was done in close collaboration with the author, whose English comprehension is excellent and who has I hope helped prevent me from betraying too often his intended meaning. In part 1, I have added a few notes to clarify some interesting points raised by the first reviewers of the manuscript.

In the original French version, biblical quotes were drawn from a French edition of the Jerusalem Bible, but the New Testament quotations were often made fresh by the author in order to provide a more literal rendition of the Greek text. In the present English translation, all scriptural citations have been updated to follow the Catholic edition of the NRSV. In some places where an alternate translation was more appropriate for the text, I have noted this in a parenthetical citation or have added an explanatory note.

Finally, my special thanks go to Dan Keating for his tremendous help editing and formatting the text, to Elena Leontjeva for her corrections and helpful suggestions, and to Michael Centore for his encouragement and for the efforts he deployed to find a suitable home in the United States for Jean-Miguel Garrigues's *God without the Idea of Evil*.

Gregory Casprini, O.S.B.
Saint Benedict's Monastery, Palendriai, Lithuania

Introduction

To provide a basis for the contemplation of the mystery of the innocence of God, I intend to use the icon of the Trinity. This particular type of icon existed long before the one Saint Andrei Rublev painted in Russia. In the Eastern tradition it has a title, because icons are generally marked with an inscription. But the title of this one is not the *Holy Trinity*. It is impossible to represent the Trinity directly in an icon. Icons always express themselves through the mediation of the Incarnation; it is always through Christ and his saints, through the human element in God's revelation, that icons convey their message. That is why this icon only represents the Trinity in a mysterious, indirect way. Its title in the Eastern tradition is the "hospitality of Abraham," since its historical basis is the hospitality given by Abraham to the three mysterious figures who paid him a visit at the Oak of Mamre. The fathers of the church often reflected on these three mysterious personages who accomplished the visit of the "Angel of the Lord," that is to say, of the Lord himself to Abraham. The fathers tended to see this as a foreshadowing of the Trinity. Thus the icon of Abraham's hospitality, of Abraham welcoming God as if he were a pilgrim, represented by these three visiting angels, has become the icon of the Trinity as we know it (see figure 1).

Figure 1. Icon of the Hospitality of Abraham, by Andrei Rublev

Rublev's icon is not simply the representation of Abraham's hospitality. The proof of this is that it contains, as it were, two departures from the literal exactitude of the story in Genesis. These two departures from the text concern that which, in Rublev's icon, has come to be of central importance. In previous icons of this type, it is usually possible to perceive on the table prepared for the three visitors wheat cakes and a calf, which were the two dishes Abraham served his guests according to the text of Genesis. But in the icon of Rublev, which subsequently became the archetype of this group of icons, there is, in the middle of the table, neither wheat cakes nor a calf but instead a cup, of which Genesis makes absolutely no mention. In the cup, there is something difficult to discern with the naked eye and even more difficult to see in reproductions. But it would seem that when examining the contents of the cup with a magnifying glass, one perceives a lamb rather than a calf.

A cup containing a lamb. I would like to propose this image as the oriental basis for our contemplation of the mystery of the Lamb. At the heart of the mystery of the Trinity there is the Lamb, a Lamb contained in a cup. This is what we will be contemplating through the texts of Holy Scripture, and in the light of the spiritual understanding that we can draw from the church fathers and the theology of Saint Thomas Aquinas.

The other iconographic basis to keep before our eyes is the fresco of the Blessed Fra Angelico, a Dominican brother of the San Marco Convent in Florence. He too was an iconographer, and his work is practically contemporary with that of Rublev. He painted an icon for the cell of each brother. And thus all the cells in the San Marco Convent have an icon. This icon entirely covers the back wall of the cell and constitutes the background of the room. The cells are small, and thus each brother was placed in the presence of an icon representing Christ at different moments of his life, and especially in scenes related to the Passion and the Resurrection. At the same time the icons depict Saint Dominic, who is either seated at the foot of the cross or meditating on the mystery of the Passion. One icon represents Saint Dominic contemplating Christ as he was mocked by the soldiers in the courtyards of the high priest and of the Roman praetorium.

But here too, because the Blessed Angelico, like Andrei Rublev, was an authentic iconographer and not simply a religious painter, the historical reality itself becomes a kind of epiphany allowing us to enter into the eternal mystery. Christ was scourged and then, out of mockery, covered in a purple-colored robe; it was the cape or mantle worn by the Roman soldiers, which they placed on Jesus's shoulders to deride him because he was about to be condemned as the King of the Jews and because purple was the royal or imperial color. In the Fra Angelico icon, however, Christ is enveloped not in purple but in white. He wears a white, resplendent garment.

We see here not a simple historical representation of the scene of Christ being subjected to mockery but instead Christ depicted in majesty, the Christ of the Transfiguration, or of the Resurrection. Or perhaps this may even be Christ as the eternal image of the Father, of thrice-holy God, since we see him seated on a throne. The throne itself is raised up on a platform in front of a tapestry that underlines even more the impression of royalty conveyed by the scene. Nothing here evokes the courtyard of the high priest or of Pilate. Christ is sitting majestically as the most holy God, holding in his right hand a reed, which in the gospel episode was a sign of derision but which becomes here a royal scepter. In his left hand he has the terrestrial globe. Indeed, he holds the world and the entire universe in his hand, for he is the One in whom all things were created. But this Christ sitting in majesty is at the same time the Christ subjected to mockery. He bears on his head the crown of thorns and his eyes are blindfolded. In the icon, it is this last touch that is perhaps the most mysterious. His eyes are blindfolded, but his face shines transparently through the veil, a bit like in the Shroud of Turin. One can perceive his eyes and nose. And his eyes are closed. (See the image on the cover of the book.)

This God of majesty has been blindfolded (the blindfolding is mentioned explicitly in Mark 14:65 and Luke 22:64). Why have they done this? They have blindfolded him to prevent him from seeing, or from being able to see, the ones who are hitting him. "Prophesy! Say who it is that struck you," they say, as they hit him with reeds, spit on him, and slap him. "Who is it that struck you?" The God of majesty, who holds the entire world in his hand, is blindfolded with regard to the mystery of evil that is attacking him. Revolving around him we see a hateful round of instruments, as well as hands that are striking him. In the icon these hands do not belong to a body; we see no people but only hands: he is being attacked by as many as four hands, hands without bodies, hands that float in the air without being attached to a body. One of those hands carries a stick, while the others are empty. There is only one human face, but this face too is without a body. It is the face of a man, no doubt one of the soldiers: he lifts his hat, because the gospel text says, "they saluted Him," making mock gestures of reverence as before a king while striking him. The human head with a raised hat, this man who spits on Christ, is also without a body. Christ enthroned in majesty is only surrounded by a horrible set of violent hands, and by this head that spits forth at the mouth.

Here again, as with the Trinity icon, we are transported from a historical event to a kind of eternal event concerning the mystery of God himself, the thrice-holy Lord who in this icon radiates an immense majesty, an immense serenity. This is not a Christ who is suffering, in the way that the Lord experienced human suffering at that particular moment in time, but it is in actual fact the same deity appearing in the guise of humanity, as in the Byzantine icons. And it is this same divine being who is assailed by the evil of the world. We have here not just the hostility of this cohort of soldiers who derisively attacked Christ in the high priest's courtyard. The hostile characters in this scene have been totally depersonalized in order to represent the evil of all mankind, the evil of all time, which revolts against and assails the mystery of God. There is something else totally new and original here, and in this Fra Angelico proves himself to be a truly inspired iconographer, just as Rublev did when he depicted his cup containing a Lamb. Angelico, for his part, is inspired to show us that his God of majesty is absolutely blind to evil. In his painting the Lord is blindfolded. He can in no way see evil. This fact will constitute the very center of the mystery into which we are about to enter. When the soldiers say to Jesus, "Who is it that struck you?" he cannot see. This amazing historical detail becomes here a metaphysical and theological manifestation of the divinity itself, a manifestation that appears on the serene, majestically meek face of the Lamb who is led to the slaughterhouse and who opens neither his mouth nor his eyes.

That which the East, in Rublev's icon, gives us to contemplate concerning the mystery of the origins, with a cup containing the Lamb even before the foundation of the world, is now revealed to us, in the West, in both its historical and permanent actualization, thanks to the painting of Fra Angelico. For, as Pascal puts it, "Christ undergoes agony until the end of the world." Through Jesus Christ's historical agony, which lasted for only a brief interval of time, we see in this fresco a manifestation of the mysterious agony of the love of a God who has been scorned and rejected but who nonetheless receives and takes upon himself in the divine majesty of his holiness the contradiction caused by the unacceptable evil of sin. Through all of this, God remains "blind" in relation to evil, for he can in no way "conceive" it. According to the astounding expression of Saint Thomas Aquinas, "God has no idea of evil."

"Prophesy! Who is it that struck you?" No, God can neither "state nor conceive" moral evil in a "divine idea." This evil is something inconceivable and unacceptable for him but also something that he accepts victoriously (in order to vanquish and overcome it) in a superabundance of love for mankind. God can neither predict nor even conceive an idea of this evil, because he himself is ontologically foreign to it and infinitely removed from it. He has nothing, absolutely nothing, to do with evil; he is in no way in league with it, either actively or passively, directly or indirectly. He is totally foreign to evil: and yet this evil assails him, raising its hand against his divine majesty and spitting into his face, which is radiant with glory.

At the feet of Christ enthroned in his divine majesty but whose face has been subjected to insult and scorn, we see, in this icon, Saint Dominic and the Virgin Mary. Surprisingly, these two figures do not contemplate the depicted scene as a historical event. In other icons of the Saint Marco Convent, especially in the crucifixion scenes, Saint Dominic kneels or stands, his arms encircling the cross, which he literally embraces and hugs against himself. Here, on the contrary, we see Dominic sitting outside the overall context of the icon, with a book open on his lap, reading very quietly as if nothing were happening. Nonetheless, as he reads, he is contemplating and meditating on the wisdom of God, who, in the mystery of the Lamb, was speechless and blind in the face of evil. Mary is sitting on the other side. She too is meditating, her head resting on one hand. She is without a book because she does not need one, having given birth to the Lamb. She carries within herself the book of the Christ's Incarnation, the Incarnation of which she is the privileged witness. And thus, these two figures, Saint Dominic and Mary, very calmly seated one step lower than the throne, meditate on the divine mystery that was accomplished in time, once and for all, the mystery around which, according to the motto of the Carthusian order, all history revolves. The cross is the immobile axis around which the entire world revolves: *stat crux dum volvitur orbis*.

Let us therefore remain continually in contemplation before these two icons. Whenever our discourse becomes too abstract, we must return to the simple intuition offered by these images. The icons propose a simple primary visual intuition, which speech then attempts to dissect, describe, and analyze but which it must be careful not to destroy in the process.

Saint Andrei Rublev's icon introduces us into what the church fathers call the "mysterious counsel of the Trinity." It is there that the divine design is decided by the three divine persons together. It is the design of God our creator and Father, who chose us even before the world came into existence. It is he who loved us in his Son, and who enveloped us in the blessings of his Spirit. Saint Andrei Rublev's icon suggests to us that this divine plan, which is the source of all things, takes on, at its very origin in the heart of the Trinity, the precise form of the Lamb.

PART ONE

The Mystery

The innocent benevolence of the creative design of the Father

God has no idea of evil.
—Saint Thomas Aquinas,
Summa Theologiae I, q. 15, a. 3, ad. 1

There is nothing future for God.
—Saint Thomas Aquinas,
I Sent. dist. 38, q. 1, ad. 5um

CHAPTER ONE

The Omnipotence of the Father

At the beginning of the creed each one of us proclaims, "I believe in God, the Father Almighty." An Almighty Father! Somehow these two words appear to contradict each other. The word *Father* is indeed charged with ambiguity, but when it resonates in our hearts, even if only with a kind of sad nostalgia, in the case of those who have suffered from negative experiences related to human parenthood, this word *Father* still carries a promise of goodness, mercy, and kindness. Consequently, a God who is an Almighty Father, a Father whose goodness is supported by his omnipotence, should offer us a life that is full of wonder and delight. But when the creed goes on to declare that this Almighty Father is the creator of heaven and earth, we are almost inevitably driven to ask in astonishment: "How comes it then, that our world is not a paradise?" And this can lead us to wonder which of the two words, *Father* or *Almighty*, contains a lie or is unable to fulfill its promise.

Indeed, here we encounter two possible temptations against the faith: either we believe that Almighty God is not really a Father, that is to say, that he is not really and totally a God of goodness and mercy, since the world seems to follow its own course, involving in particular the scandal of evil that constantly clutches at our throat; or we grant that God truly is a Father and that he really does want the best for us, but we suspect that he is not really "all-powerful" but that something escapes him and that his governing of creation is not entirely effective in reality.

Both these temptations are quite present in modern-day culture, which oscillates between two suspicions about God. The first is the idea of a "sadistic" God who is the enemy of man and who is jealous of him. We find here the projection onto God of all our images of bad paternity, due to all the failures of family and parenthood, which are so common in our everyday life. It is not surprising that all the sins, failures, and distortions arising from relationships between parents and children have been projected and heaped onto the face of God. The opposite suspicion is to think of God as indeed a father (or even a grandfather!) who is good and well-meaning but who is powerless or impotent, a God whose will of salvation is more a feeble wish than a real and victorious commitment for the good of mankind. Of such a God the only thing that it would be possible to say is that "he is dead"!

Yet when we profess our faith in the Father Almighty, these two words are inseparable; they draw their strength, as it were, one from the other. At the beginning of the creed, omnipotence is attributed to God the Father. It might have seemed more natural to assign this trait directly to God the creator by saying, for example, "We believe in God the Father, who is the Almighty creator of heaven and earth." It is easier for us to believe in the omnipotence of God in creation than to believe in the omnipotence of God in his paternity, that is, in his providence, in the care that he exercises on our behalf, in his manner of accompanying us in our daily lives. To assign omnipotence to God in his paternity is somewhat of a challenge, or even a provocation. It is easier for us to believe in the omnipotence of God in creation in our day and age, when we know much better the immensity of the cosmos as well as the intricately perfect way in which matter is constituted. From the infinitely large to the infinitely small, we sense God's omnipotence at work; but this omnipotence seems ridiculously impotent when it comes to our lives and to the unfolding of our daily existence. There, indeed, the omnipotence of God seems to suffer an eclipse, even as it continues to shine on the rest of the universe. But it is precisely in our day-to-day existence that we most desperately seek the face of God the Father. However, when we think we have found him, we can have the impression of confronting either the impotence of an old man, sweet-faced and benevolent but whose arms are tired, or the enigmatic face of a cold omnipotence that we may be tempted to accuse of total indifference or even of cruelty.

The Face of the Father

To discover the face of God the Father we will need to retrace all the stages through which the Lord has accompanied man throughout the entire course of his history. This will enable us to discern more and more the face of God as our Father while helping us determine that which is the last word concerning his omnipotence. As we proceed along this journey, our spontaneous ideas of what fatherhood and omnipotence are will probably have to undergo a transformation. These two notions, *father* and *almighty*, are very powerfully and deeply rooted in us. At the same time, because they occupy an archaic place in the development of a child's psychology, they can remain frozen at an infantile level. One can often find, even in people who are very advanced intellectually, traces of immaturity or infantilism when it comes to the way in which they perceive fatherhood or omnipotence.

We will have to purify these two concepts, a little like when we adjust the two lenses of a pair of binoculars, so that the double image through which we have been perceiving fatherhood and omnipotence can become the embossed vision of a single reality: the true face of a Father who is a father because he is all-powerful but who is all-powerful *only* in his paternity.

Let us first consider how the face of the Father emerges in God's work of creation. What specifically does the idea of a father add to our discovery of the creator? The mere fact that there is a God who is the creator does not in itself imply that creation is intended for or addressed to someone. God could have made a cosmos as an end in itself, as a perfectly accomplished masterpiece, like a beautiful piece of clockwork, made exclusively for his glory, as the reflection of his power and might. But this creation would not have been addressed to someone who is called to enter into a personal relationship with God. The face of the Father in creation appears when it is revealed as *an inheritance*. Then it no longer appears as a cosmos with its end in itself but as a gift, as something that is intended for someone who is an heir. It is not by chance that Jesus, in the parable of the prodigal son (Luke 15:11–32), which is an illustration of original sin, presents the prodigal son as asking of his father, "Father, give me the share of the property that will belong to me"; that is to say, give me the creation but the creation without you, so that I can use it and enjoy it apart, by myself and for myself, far away from you.

The Message of That Which Is Transitory or Ephemeral

At certain privileged moments, creation really does seem to present itself to us as a legacy. At times we can be captivated by a splendid landscape or a seascape, by mountains or by a vast rolling countryside, by a magnificent sunset, or by the splendor of a night sky filled with stars. The spectacle of all this beauty can inspire us to glorify the creator. Sometimes at these same moments, when the grandeur and the majestic beauty of the creator are manifested, we also perceive a gesture that seems to be addressed to us personally. It is almost as if someone is smiling at us, and waving his hand, or even nodding to us with a touch of humor from behind the veil of so much beauty and perfection. And strangely enough, it is precisely the most ephemeral and transitory aspects of creation that tend to shimmer in this way, conveying a message from the One who is behind the veil, dwelling in the world of the invisible. Had he wanted to, God could have created an immobile or perfectly repetitive world, closed in upon itself, with each element accomplishing its own circular movement in an entirely predictable and necessary manner. But we sense that there is something else at work in creation, especially in the mystery of change and of time. Today's sunset, for example, has something unique about it, because we will never see the likes of it again. Of course, tomorrow there will be another sunset, but it will not be the same one. To borrow a phrase from Vigny, in this particular sunset we love "that which will never be twice seen."

The ephemeral aspect of the world carries a definite message. It tells us that creation, far from being a system hermetically closed in upon itself, is the bearer of a higher secret that can only be deciphered by our liberty. We have here something very poignant: beings who are endowed with freedom, who are immersed in time, and who experience nonrepetitive change or evolution in their own human existence can also perceive the transitory, nonrepetitive aspects that already exist in the inanimate creation itself, in the cosmos. This message of the ephemeral indicates that our world, far from being a completely closed system, is capable of giving a faintly perceptible sign to our liberty, whose sense of time is marked by that which is new and unpredictable. Becoming aware of the world's transitory character can be an extremely lacerating experience because although we would naturally like to prolong forever our moments of happiness, we sense at the same time that the essence of beauty as it exists in this world resides precisely in its fleetingness. The fleeting nature of things shows that creation, even in its most immutable and serene aspects, is primarily a pledge or a token given to our liberty that is in constant motion, searching continually, and never allowing itself to be imprisoned in any cosmic determinism.

This is how we ought to understand the chaotic lack of order (in Hebrew, *tohu-bohu*) found in creation and which we sometimes experience so painfully. This tohu-bohu reminds us that material creation is not made for itself but for us humans beings. It is a legacy, and as such, it has been prepared in order to be placed at the disposal of those who are called to inherit it. In other words, it has been made so that it can be used, serving as a path for our liberty. The elements of chaos or incompleteness, or tohu-bohu — to borrow from the first words of the book of Genesis (1:2) — show that creation has not yet reached its final order. God the creator has not yet given this definitive order because he wants creation to be a road leading to God the Father, a road for the liberty of men, who are called by divine grace to participate in the unpredictable order of love. Thus the Father's face can already be vaguely discerned in the incompleteness of creation. We must not be afraid of this transient aspect of creation, especially today, when human technology is seeking to more and more efficiently make use of the resources of the earth.

We must try to avoid confusion in considering the ecological problems that are so often an issue today. We must distinguish here between two different points of view. It is one thing to militate in favor of a rational and humane use of the cosmos, a use that respects the wholesome integrity of

God's creation while seeking to ensure justice among men by distributing and using natural resources in a way that fully takes into account the needs of all mankind in its present and future generations. It is another thing to systematically lament and grieve over any and all of the inevitable wear and tear imposed on the cosmos when some of its primary resources are depleted by technology in an effort to help the human community free itself gradually from the strenuous conditioning of nature. The cosmos is intended to be, in a certain sense, the chrysalis of man, ushering in the new man. In its present state the cosmos is not meant to be our definitive home. Along with Psalm 102 we can sing the praises of God who is to fold away the heavens and the earth like a worn-out garment. The book of Revelation shows us how this worn-out, tired cosmos will one day be rolled up like a scroll (Rev. 6:14), making a place for the new world that emerges suddenly, like a butterfly coming out of its cocoon, and that is re-created, starting with the "new man," with man in perfect communion with God and with his fellow human beings.

A Creation for Man

God is a Father even before being the creator: he adopts the liberty of those whom he is going to create, so that this liberty can become the last and final word of the cosmos. Man is not made in order to be inserted like a cog in the great cosmic wheel; he is not simply placed in the service of what are called the natural laws (as if these laws and the present state of the cosmos were destined to last forever). This is not so, for as Saint Paul teaches us (1 Cor. 13:18), the only thing that will never pass away is love, which sets human liberty free so that it can respond to God. Love is like the indestructible diamond against which the Lord will measure all things. We need not be afraid to place the material world in the service of justice and love, and to use it up, so to speak, in the accomplishment of this task. It is a bit like at the end of Jules Verne's novel *Around the World in Eighty Days*: when the boat returns from America to Europe, the crew accelerates so much that they use up all the fuel, and then they resort to burning almost the entire vessel in order to reach the goal, which is to bring the navigator to his destination.

This corresponds to the vision of creation found in the fathers of the church, notably in the writings of Saint Irenaeus of Lyons. Man is made to absorb, in a certain sense, the cosmos. He himself, through the exercise of his liberty, which is called by grace to enter into communion with God, is like the Tree of Life in paradise as depicted in Genesis. He plunges his roots into all of the conditions and preconditions of this cosmos. For him these are resources that he must utilize in the most advantageous way possible but from which he must also liberate himself by taking everything up into himself. The law that must regulate this integration is man in communion with his brothers and sisters and with God, not some merely cosmic law. The entire order of the cosmos, including the animals, is, according to Genesis (2:3), radically submitted to man and to his growth.[1] Here we need to refute vegetarianism: not, of course, as a dietary principle, which many people, including some Christians, can find healthy and legitimate, but as an ideology that considers it a scandal that men eat animals and disturb in this way the order of creation. First of all, animals were eating one another long before the appearance of man and original sin. In the great primeval oceans, big fish were already eating little fish. Animal species have long been appearing and disappearing, because all of that was made not to last but to pass away. But man, and man alone, must see to it that this creation does not pass away in vain. Paul in Romans (8:19–22) teaches that the natural wearing away of the cosmos, along with the supplementary wearing away imposed on it by human liberty, must not occur in vain, as a pure loss. Instead it must produce a fruit of immortality, that of "the glorious liberty of the children of God." Love will never pass away.

The World, a Chrysalis of Liberty

It is the superior and final goals of the ethical order that constitute the fundamental laws from which the new world must come. We must not be frightened by the fact that this old world is wearing away; it was made for that. This does not mean that we should treat the world as if it were a mere stage set that we could pass through with our liberty without committing ourselves or getting involved. In our lives, the world is not a simple backdrop in a theater. On the contrary, for our liberty, called and destined to enter into a communion of love, this world is what the nourishing loam is to a tree, or what the chrysalis is to the butterfly. Indeed, like the butterfly before it emerges from its chrysalis, man must entirely absorb the richness of his life-sustaining environment constituted by the cosmos.

Eternal life begins to come into play during this present life, in this world, but its activity is so intense that it wears out the cosmos to the point of making it crack. But we will emerge from it entirely transformed because, to repeat the metaphor, *the substance of the chrysalis will be taken up into the caterpillar, and the caterpillar will become a butterfly.*

Man must cause this world to pass, not into vanity, but into love, charity, *agape*. Creation is the adventure of nature becoming history — the history of human liberty that feeds, as it were, on the inorganic, plant, and animal world. Man, like unto a tree, must all at once be rooted in the earth and climb toward the heavens. His first experience of communion is like that of a tree's roots with the earth, but ultimately it becomes similar to that of a tree's branches and leaves with the sky and air.

The face of God the Father manifests itself in this transient character of the cosmos, a transience that gives the universe all its heartrending beauty. Christians should consider themselves deliverers or "freedom guides" in this world that is held prisoner by the vanity of sin; somewhat like during the German occupation of France, when "freedom guides" helped the persecuted pass over the border and escape to liberty. Christians are not here to eternally perpetuate this world, and chapter 11 of the Epistle to the Hebrews seeks to remind us of that. The Christian is someone who passes through, and who is not afraid to pass because he has learned the art of passing through in love. One of the most beautiful things that the Father teaches Christians is to pass successively through time: to first be young and then adults, to grow old and die, and to go through these different stages in love and in joy. Anyone who learns to do this is able to radiate this love and joy to those around him, because he has given up the nostalgic myth of an immobile creation. Christians gradually discover that God is the Almighty Father precisely insofar as he accompanies his children in this passage rather than seeking to give them a form of happiness scaled down to their finite human proportions in a world that continues eternally. The omnipotence of the Father appears in the fact that he decided to elevate man and introduce him into a personal communion with himself rather than leave him as a cog among the elements of a world, no matter how perfect that world might be. Consequently, this world of ours must experience "the sufferings of childbirth," due to the liberty of man. Today this liberty is expressing itself, among other things, through technological development, which is subjecting the material world to fatigue and exhaustion.

All this should open Christians to an authentic wisdom of love turned toward hope. We are asked to bear witness concerning the true face of the Father. The manner in which we make use of this world should not only pay tribute to the creator. Primarily it should be an expression of man's relationship with God the Father, an offering of gratitude and service on behalf of the whole human family, given to the One "from whom every family in heaven and on earth takes its name" (Eph. 3:15). Now this family is constituted and unified by passing to the Father. And thus we can say with Paul that if our present earthly abode is falling into ruin, we know that God, at the same time, is building our eternal home (2 Cor. 5:1). It is with the elements of our old world that the new world is being built, not by an eternal prolongation of the old order, but according to a final and definitive order constituted by the order of love.

Man: The Heir of the Creator

To shed more light on this we must recall the story of creation in Genesis. When God creates the cosmos, starting with the separation of light from darkness and going up to the creation of the animals, he proceeds by giving orders. The Genesis story uses imperative sentences: "let there be light"; "let the earth put forth plants; let the waters and the earth bring forth animals," and so on. When a verb is in the imperative mood, the speaker who gives the order does not have to appear personally. His face does not have to be shown. Indeed, his power is manifested and also his intelligence (because one can realize if an order is foolish or intelligent), but neither his face nor his person is revealed. There is no better way to remain anonymous and aloof, no better way to avoid entering into personal communion, than to proceed by giving orders.

But on the sixth day, when God creates man, he gives an order to himself, or rather, he takes counsel and deliberates with himself. He does not say, "Let man come into existence," but instead: "Let us make humankind in our image, according to our likeness; and let them have dominion over the fish of the sea, and over the birds of the air, and over the cattle, and over all the wild animals of the earth" (Gen. 1:26). When God creates man, he acts as the creator only inasmuch as he is a Father. The creation of man is not simply the creation of an additional element of the cosmos among others; it expresses a design of grace, manifesting the desire of God's heart. God deliberates with himself. God speaks in the first person. God commits himself as a subject of the sentence, as the protagonist in a love story. "Let us make humankind in our image," says he. And he adds, "according to our likeness." At the center of the world, God introduces not just one additional reality, but the reflection of his own face, in an interpersonal communion. And thus in man the Lord reveals his face as a Father. For in man the omnipotence of the creative act culminates, as it were, in the omnipotence of fatherhood. When he introduces man into the world, God imprints on him his own image, that is to say, the freedom of the Holy Spirit. He breathes the Spirit into man, so that man can respond by accepting to enter into the communion of grace that will give him immortal life. Man, even as he first appears in prehistoric times, despite all the fragility that obliges him to hide in caves in order to escape the attacks of wild animals, already carries within himself this spark through which he feels called to a destiny entirely different from that of the rest of the cosmos, which he is called to dominate. Has not man already survived a great many of the animal species that surrounded him when he first appeared?

In creating man, the creator manifests himself as the Father who gives an inheritance. Creation is the inheritance of God given to man. Henceforth everything depends on the reception of this inheritance. Creation, however, is only a part of the inheritance that God has promised to man. Indeed, he has enabled man to dominate, by his liberty and by his intelligence, the entire material universe. But in creating him according to his image and likeness, God has given him something much more precious. He has given him his own resemblance, that is, the capacity to live and grow in a communion of love with him. This is God's secret: he gives himself as a legacy to man. It is in this that he really is a Father. But man who emerges into liberty has the ability to situate himself in two different ways. On the one hand, he can seize creation as the portion of the inheritance to which he feels entitled and which he thinks God owes him. In this case he will use his liberty as a way of exploiting and devastating the world. On the other hand, he can resolve to place at the center of the growth of his liberty the desire to enter into possession of the entire inheritance and not to appropriate any part of it to himself by detaching it from the most precious good, which is God himself. The error of original sin was a deviation of the heart and not just an intellectual error. Jesus illustrated this very well in the parable of the prodigal son. God wanted to give man the entire inheritance, while the prodigal son asks to receive "his portion of the inheritance." But what part of the inheritance? The inheritance is indivisible because it is given in the love of the Father, and it is constituted by and includes the Father himself, who declared to the elder son of the parable, "You are always with me, and all that is mine is yours."

Two Ways Liberty Can Grow

In the garden of paradise, the two aspects of our liberty, the luminous aspect and the darker, shadier aspect, are represented in the story of Genesis by the image of two trees: the Tree of Life and the Tree of the Knowledge of Good and Evil. Man in his liberty stands at the center of the entire creation that he receives from God as an inheritance. Human liberty stands there like a tree that plunges its roots into the earth for nourishment and then climbs up toward communion with the heavens, where the oxygen of divine grace causes it to grow in love. The Tree of Life represents the liberty to which God was calling man, a liberty that was surrounded by the Lord's love and grace so that it could grow by integrating more and more the partial goods of creation into a communion with the supreme good, which is God. The liberty of Adam, the first man, promised to be an extraordinary adventure. It could have led to an entirely different history of mankind, without original sin. We must not think that such a history would have been more dull and less filled with adventure than our own. It would have been rather less dominated by cosmic conditioning and richer in events inspired by the unpredictable spontaneity of love. The more our liberty is in communion with love in its divine source, the freer it is, not functioning in a predetermined, automatic way, but fully imaginative and inventive. For God cannot be jealous of our initiatives in accomplishing a good of which he is the primary source.

Next to the Tree of Life, which according to the design of the Father represented the gift of the entire inheritance, there was another tree; or perhaps, rather than a different tree, the mere shadow of the Tree of Life. For in the sphere of creation, the divine light of grace entails the possibility that the liberty that it has illuminated will cast a shadow. The potentially dark side of created liberty, which has not yet fully entered into communion with God, is symbolized by the Tree of the Knowledge of Good and Evil. It was possible for man to misuse (and he did in fact misuse) his God-given liberty to grow and progress in the good. It was possible for him to misuse his ability to subordinate a lower good to a higher one. Freedom of "choice" does not necessarily have to imply a choice between good and evil; freedom is primarily a choice between that which is good and that which is best: Jesus during his life was constantly making choices, but he never chose between good and evil because he was the son of God, and God has no idea of evil.

It was possible for man, who at the time of his creation was like a child, to be "naughty," to act according to his own whims. But we must remember that although the capricious whims, which generally constitute the sins of the children, can seem small and insignificant in their material object, they can nonetheless have grave consequences if they inflect the fundamental inclination of liberty in its primary orientation to its goal. In our children, we must not minimize the importance of such things, especially when they affect the trust and the communion existing in the relationship with their parents. This, of course, in no way implies that parents should arbitrarily require anything and everything from their children, with the risk of exasperating them, as Saint Paul warns. On the contrary, parents can expect trust and communion from their children only inasmuch as their paternity is a true reflection of divine fatherhood. The capriciousness of original sin consisted in having sought to jump ahead of God's gift. Man resolved to take his liberty entirely into his own hands, deciding that he had in himself sufficient criteria for discerning and determining that which is good, his ultimate goal, so that he could be free to manage by himself, independently, the portion of the inheritance that is this world. Man was in fact called to "dominate" the world by opening himself up, step by step, to a greater good, learning from God to find happiness and contentment in more universal goods. This is the very essence of virtue, and it would have enabled man to grow in himself and attain higher and greater goods, higher and greater goals. But instead of doing this, man decided that he was capable of knowing and setting up for himself the sufficient measure of what is good. From that moment on he conceived the idea of evil, because, inevitably, the good adopted by man as the ultimate principle and goal of his liberty was, in fact, only a partial good, which was not oriented to the Father and which was therefore not the entire inheritance. Instead, man began to idolize his immediate pleasure, imagining that this could bring him the ultimate happiness, which, in fact, resides only in communion with God. This is how a teacher like Saint Irenaeus interprets the temptation, "you will be like unto gods." He did not see in original sin a revolt of pride in man (i.e., in Adam) similar to that of Prometheus, rising up against God to take his place. Nothing in the Genesis narrative allows us to infer such a thing. One has only to watch Adam and Eve trembling and ashamed when God appears after the fault. No, Adam and Eve are not like Prometheus; nor is Satan himself for that matter. Biblical sin is free from any Promethean or Manichaean concept.

Our first parents are presented by Saint Irenaeus as children who maliciously wanted to show off their cleverness. The parable of the prodigal son is really the best exegesis of original sin. Adam and Eve seized the heritage with their own hands, and because it was not the entire inheritance, they in fact devastated it and laid it to waste. Death thus made its entry, and everything was reduced to vanity, everything turned out to be pure loss, as man devoured his own capital. Jesus said of the prodigal son that after having wasted everything, he fell under the domination of an evil master (Satan) and was reduced to desperately wanting to nourish himself with pig feed. All this indicates the degree to which he had degraded himself in his dignity as heir.

The Pedagogy of the Father

God is a Father because he did not originally give man an arbitrary commandment, just to see whether or not he would be obedient. God is not interested in obedience as a pure formality. True parents never give arbitrary orders to their sons and daughters; they indicate to their children that which is authentically good for them. Such is the kind of obedience that real paternity requires. And thus God said to Adam, "If you eat the fruit of the Tree of the Knowledge of Good and Evil," that is, if you transform into a desire for self-sufficiency your liberty of communion, in which you are still very small and in which you have to learn so much about love before sampling immortality in a love that does not pass away, if you change this liberty into a choice for total autonomy, believing you can fend for yourself, taking the world into your own hands so as to find all your happiness therein, then "you will surely die." No, it is not I who will put you to death as a punishment, but you yourself will waste away your inheritance, you will reduce everything to naught, to vanity. Instead of growing and taking part in the fruit of the Tree of Life, which *is* immortality, you will know the bitter taste of fatigue, suffering, and destruction unto death. These are not punishments that God invented and established in advance, arbitrarily. The Lord's justice is immanent to our liberty; it operates from the inside of our free choices. It is man who introduced death into the world; it is man who became his own executioner; it is man who condemned himself to so much fatigue, to all this suffering; it is man who in a certain sense committed suicide out of pure foolishness. These evils are not curses falling from the sky due to the wrath of a sovereign angry at subjects who have not obeyed his orders. God really wanted to give man the entire inheritance. But in order for the liberty of man to enter into communion with the entire inheritance, he needed to allow himself, as Saint Irenaeus said, to become gradually accustomed to the immortal love that is God.

We know practically nothing about the road that the liberty of an unfallen Adam might have taken, but we do know something about the Virgin Mary; in her, we see a liberty that is not turned toward the knowledge of good and evil but that has nevertheless gone through all the deaths to the self required in order to grow in love. Mary's liberty passed through all the thresholds necessary for a journey in faith. This shows that the history of a person's liberty can be an amazing adventure without having to go through any oscillations between good and evil. Even without sin, the mere fact of passing from the state of being a creature of God to that of communion with the Father and to the discovery of the entire heritage he has prepared is still something that is all at once exhilarating and terribly daunting. The design of the Father, because it involved filial adoption through grace and the progressive education of persons gifted with liberty, necessarily had to be a "drama" in the strict sense of the word, that is, an adventure of liberty. But it did not necessarily have to be a tragedy. It is we who have changed the "drama" of liberty into the tragedy of sin.

The Father is thus bound, in a certain sense, by his design because he cannot suppress the liberty of his children, even when that liberty turns bad. He could not suppress it without removing at the same time the possibility of communion with the entire inheritance. And thus after the fall, the human race, which God was endeavoring to lead, was only living under a degraded form of liberty, vacillating between good and evil, through flesh and blood, through suffering and covenants,[2] through ruptures and reconciliations. Such was the human condition until the coming of Jesus Christ, who died in order to take upon himself our liberty, which had gone astray and fallen into death. He took it upon himself so that he could reinfuse it with the life of the Spirit. For it is the Spirit who gives once again that living communion with the Father, reinstating the law of growth that God had given to the liberty of Adam in order to lead him to immortality. However, that which was easily accomplished in the beginning, when God simply blew the breath of life into the nostrils of the first Adam, could only be accomplished for man in his present condition, from the very depths of the decadence into which his liberty has fallen. It is only through the last breath of Christ, the second or last Adam who made himself obedient unto death, that God could infuse his Spirit of love into the heart of man.

Christians ought to bear witness before the world to the fact that the omnipotence of God resides entirely in his paternity. The Father gives us the Spirit of sonship, which delivers us from the type of liberty that vacillates between good and evil, keeping us in a state of forgetfulness with regard to evil. Our problem is not primarily to choose good and avoid evil. When we conceive an evil thought, we will perhaps still choose the good 99 percent of the time, but sooner or later a hundredth time will come when we will choose evil. If the idea of evil enters the mind of man, it is a sign that the communion with God in the Spirit is already missing. The vacuum left by the absence of communion with God is filled by a lie, because sin is nothing but a lie concerning our true good and our true joy.

But insofar as we discover that the true authentic liberty is a liberty of communion in love, we become capable of restoring in the church the unity of the human race. In this way we can serve as a rallying point in this divided world made up of the descendants of Adam.

It is at this point that Christians can say: We know the last word of the omnipotence of God, and that word is his paternity; the final word is the loving face of our heavenly Father. The heart of the Father consists in a love that wants to do nothing without man. The Father, in his love, wants to give man the entire legacy, the full inheritance of immortal happiness through communion with him, in his presence. If we can succeed in showing others, through our own way of life, all the greatness of the inheritance that the Father has promised, then people will perhaps begin to realize that the apparent silence, the apparent impotence of God in this world and in our lives, is on the contrary a passion, the passion of an all-powerful, almighty love, stronger than all the power that God has deployed in creation. God wants to re-create the world, he wants to establish a world where there will be no more suffering or death, but he only wants to make all things new starting from the basis of our liberty, from the indestructible diamond of a love that will never pass away, because it is the heart of the Father.

God in the Present Moment of Our Liberty

God is the Father Almighty because he does not plan for or program the unexpected. And the unexpected is constituted by the liberty of his children. God is a Father but not at all in the manner of those parents who when their child is still in the cradle already say of him things like, "He is going to attend the academy of sciences," fixing in advance the path of his liberty. God wants for us only the treasure of love that is in his heart. He wants us to find our happiness in the good, but that good is like a pure light, which, when it passes through the prism of human liberty, can take on all the colors of the rainbow. In the order of the good, there is an infinite number of possible initiatives, much more numerous and far more inventive than the initiatives in the direction of evil: the imagination of our liberty in regard to that which is good is something quite extraordinary. We are often amazed when we observe the marvelous imagination that God deployed in his creation. And nevertheless, God's will is that his benevolent design of love must pass through our imaginations and be executed by the instrument of our liberty. He wants us to play our own instruments. He does not even want to write a score or a scenario in advance that he would then simply ask us to play. There is for the Lord no such thing as a scenario written in advance. When compared with our human parenthood, God, in a manner unique to himself, lives and realizes his paternity only in the present moment of the liberty of his children.

Is it not true that mothers and fathers very often live in the future or in the past, torn between dreams and disappointments concerning their children—dreams that are often only the projection of what they themselves are or compensation for that which they would have liked to be? Later, when they feel that their children are escaping from them, they become fixated on the past, full of nostalgia for the days when the kids were young and lived with them. It is very difficult to live one's parenthood in the present. God, however, does just that: he lives his fatherhood in the present. The mystery of divine fatherhood, God's omnipotent fatherhood, is something much more difficult to understand than the power he displayed in creating the universe; and only God himself can measure how much wisdom and power he employed in that act of creation. But to nurture and bring about the budding of created liberty so that it freely opens itself up to the good is something much more difficult, and the accomplishment of this task gives proof of a much more "multifaceted" and unpredictable wisdom. It is a mystery involving birth rather than a mere mystery of creation. The New Testament readily speaks of a "birth" to describe our entry into the grace of adoption as children of God. To create, to make, or to shape is something that can be done without the maker having to get too personally involved! But to bring someone into the world, to give birth, especially to a being gifted with liberty, is a work of omnipotence infinitely greater than creating galaxies or organizing the inner structure of matter. Indeed, we are dealing here with something much more unpredictable, something to which Saint Paul in the Epistle to the Ephesians applies the term "manifold wisdom" (Eph. 3:10 NIV). It requires a manifold wisdom to indwell the multicolored character of the liberty of a human being; because it is the complex network of all our liberties that God indwells in the present moment, causing them to open to the good by a gift of grace that animates them from within. In doing this, God does not dictate the road to follow. He simply awakens our liberty to the sense of what is good. And thus as Jesus says, "My Father is still working" (John 5:17). He works in the present moment, bestowing his grace on us so that we develop a true sense of taste for the good and so that we can rejoice and find our happiness therein. God ardently desires that we enter into possession of the ultimate good that he himself is. All this amounts to, literally speaking, "the present" of his grace: a *present* in both senses of the term, because it is offered in the *present moment* and because it is a *gift*. God thus indwells in this way the liberty of man, awakening in him the instinct of that which is good, amid all the unexpected and unpredictable turnings of his actions. In this way he causes human liberty to be born, and he nourishes it by his grace.

The most fundamental characteristic of the Father Almighty is that he only sees us in the present; for him all our acts are only known in the act itself in which we accomplish them. God has no project concerning us other than the establishment of an eternal communion of love between us and him in his kingdom; he has no ideas a priori about the human paths by which we must walk toward him. The history of our liberty is known to God in the present of our acts, in divine eternity. God receives this history as our response to his love, in a thrill of joy if it culminates in a definitive communion with him or as a staggering blow to his heart in the opposite case. Divine omnipotence, which we would probably tend to imagine as a controlling grip or a divine remote-control system that endeavors to direct and orient us according to a rigorously predetermined program, proves, on the contrary, to be the providence of the eternal Lord who accompanies our liberty step by step, in this present time of our acts. God leaves the future entirely open to us. He knows us only in the present. As for the past, he sees it not in his memory, for God has no memory, since he has no past, but as recorded in us, very often as a wound that he has to heal. He only knows our future in the real moment when it becomes the present of our liberty. Today he receives us in the place where we are, in the present moment of his grace. And what about tomorrow? Well, tomorrow will only exist in reality as a new today for us! It is this *today* that God knows in the present moment of his eternity. God does not make any "projections" about the future; his omnipotence is quite different from our power, which exhausts itself in an effort to dominate the passing of time, which continually slips out of our control. The omnipotence of God is the innocence of his eternity that only attaches itself to our liberty in the present moment; his is an innocence stronger than a rock because it is not weakened by any projections about the future or by memories of the past; it can therefore open up each one of the acts produced by our liberty to the virginal newness of the Good.

The Unbearable "Best of All Possible Worlds"

But why did God the Almighty Father not create a more perfect world? Before answering this question, we need to know in relation to what we are measuring perfection. Who are the creatures capable of perceiving the world's imperfection? Does the tree feel that it is imperfect? Do animals feel imperfect? Do they sense in this world an imperfection that wounds them or deprives them of something? The answer would seem to be no. Every creature follows its natural path and appears to be at ease doing so; that is, all creatures with the exception of man: he alone perceives the imperfection of the world. It would of course be possible for us to imagine a world that had been created more perfect than our own, but the more perfect we would imagine it to be, the more we would somehow end up perceiving its imperfection, because everything depends on the criteria we choose to measure perfection. For example, it might be perfection in a world like our own but in which everything that contributes to creating human adventure or dramatic situations would be removed. We could imagine a world like ours but simply prolonged infinitely in duration, a world in which all trials and tribulations would be banished and which would go on perpetually, like a spring day that never ends. But wouldn't we very soon end up finding such a world, in the words of an American sociologist, an "air-conditioned nightmare," that is, a place in which we would feel good only because everything was conditioned and measured for us? And there precisely is the rub! The world is not made to our measure, and it is a mistake to wish to scale it down to fit the measure or size of a perfection that we have imagined. This would amount to setting up our purely human happiness as the only absolute value. But if it were possible for us to do this, we would very soon perceive how dull and stifling such a world would be.

Our world, despite all its imperfections, nonetheless offers a mysterious promise for the future, a mystery of high expectation, which makes it somehow more bearable. Whereas if we were placed in a world that had been scaled down to our measure of happiness (as if we ourselves were capable of determining what our true measure of our happiness is), we would rapidly get the impression of being locked up in prison. The real problem is this: we bear within ourselves a measure that is not commensurate with this world. This means that we can constantly ask ourselves why there is not a better world, but the best one we could imagine would most certainly turn out to be for us the least satisfactory of all. The higher we climb on the ladder of cosmic perfection, the more we perceive a kind of frustration. It is well known among sociologists and historians that frustration and dissatisfaction have never been more acute than in highly developed civilizations.

The question of the best of all possible worlds is a kind of false metaphysical infinity where one can continually go further, imagining each time a still better world. But the very "best" that the heart of man desires is not just the highest level or degree within the same world; he is thirsting for something that is qualitatively different. As the famous phrase of Rimbaud puts it: "real life is elsewhere." Man is in quest of that which comes from elsewhere, and that which is "best" is perceived to be inseparably linked with an experience of something that is from "elsewhere," something that this world, in its finite state, cannot by itself provide. The more our world is ameliorated, the more it is perfected by our civilization, the more it tends to take on a stifling aspect. This can be the case notably in places where the state has become "providence," the so-called welfare state. The asphyxiating impression given by these advanced societies is infinitely greater than that which arises from the countless sufferings of more primitive and poor nations.

We must therefore look for the world's secret in a mystery that surpasses the world, a mystery that resides precisely in the fact that it is not the best of worlds and that the best of all possible worlds does not exist. When we get to this point, we can begin to listen to the secret and silent word, which is found at the very origin of the world. This origin is the mystery of the divine will; as the Apocalypse says, "You created all things, and by your will they existed and were created" (Rev. 4:11). According to the biblical revelation, the world is suspended on the will of the creator. It does not carry in itself the knowledge of its origin and cannot say the last word about itself; it does not know its end any more than its origin. On the other hand, all that lies between its origin and its end is for men to explore, and they have never deprived themselves of the joy of doing so. Sometimes, though, it has been to their great disappointment. In the book of Ecclesiastes, the knowledge of wisdom, such as it can be cataloged by human beings, goes hand in hand with a certain experience of death. There is a mysterious and secret link between knowledge and death that the book of Ecclesiastes has admirably developed. Indeed, the mystery of the origins and of the end belong by definition to a type of wisdom that cannot be elucidated by the forces of human knowledge alone.

The Eternal Newness of the Origin

There is, at the origin, the mystery of a liberty, a creative will. In the desert, Moses experiences the burning bush, where the Lord reveals himself through his mysterious name: "I am who I am" (Exod. 3:14). For anyone else, such a name would signify a refusal to speak, a refusal to reveal oneself. But for the Lord alone, it is the only name capable of defining and expressing who he is. For any of us, responding to the question, "Who are you?" by saying, "I am who I am," would be the equivalent of a refusal to respond. God alone, in saying this, answers in the most appropriate and at the same time the most mysterious way. We have here the basic, fundamental mystery of the origin of being. Such is the fire that Moses sees in the bush. Far from consuming the bush that stands for the entire creation, this fire actually keeps it alive. It is the fire of being, the fire of the gift of life, a fire that we experience as a kindhearted mystery that causes the world to tremble. It is the presence of a person, the presence of someone standing behind a quivering veil, the presence of a quivering flame that passes through every creature.

This mystery of the divine will concerning the world is related to the Son of the Almighty Father. In calling us into existence, the Father did not content himself with a creation made for itself in the manner of a "God-watchmaker" who would manufacture all the "clockwork" of the universe and then indifferently leave it to run on its own. If there is a gift of existence, if there is a communication of a flame, it is because "He who is," the divine "I am" who revealed himself to Moses, carries within his heart a mystery of love. His will is a will of love; it is a father's blessing. Thus the mystery of creation is suspended on the breath of the love of the Father and of the Son, in their mysterious kindhearted will or design, in virtue of which we have been mentioned, even before we existed, in the depths of the divinity, the depths that only the Holy Spirit can probe (1 Cor. 2:10). God did not create us simply so that we would be his creatures; he created us in order to adopt us as his children. It is one thing when unworthy parents bring a child into the world only to abandon him to an unhappy fate. It is quite another thing when they commit themselves to their parenthood, not only giving life, but also assuming all the ultimate consequences of their paternity, recognizing as their own the child whom they have brought into the world. If there is a blessing upon us from even before the foundation of the world, it is because the creation itself is only the first act of a design of adoption. God wanted the same paternal relationship that exists between himself and his Son, in the Holy Spirit, to be communicated by grace outside of himself, so that he would be fruitful to the point of producing the entire creation out of nothing.

The creation is said to have been made *through the Son*: it comes from the Father through the Son in the Holy Spirit. This is why we cannot simply measure the perfection of creation in relation to itself, according to a criterion that would be immanent to the universe; no indeed, for there exists a cry from beyond, a cry of love that traverses all creation, a cry that is actually a dialogue that pierces through for the first time in the book of Genesis, in the mysterious use by God of the first-person plural when he says, "Let *us* make humankind in *our* image, according to *our* likeness." Until then the Lord had been giving orders: "let there be light, let the heavens be[,] . . . let the earth come into existence." But now he takes counsel with himself, advising himself, talking, as it were, to himself. In this way he reveals a mysterious set of interlocutors who take part in divine intimacy. This is what Saint Paul says in a hymn that the church sometimes sings at vespers (Eph. 1:4–5): "He chose us in Christ before the foundation of the world to be holy and blameless before him in love. He destined us for adoption as his children through Jesus Christ, according to the good pleasure of his will." Crossing through creation from its very origin, there is the last word of creation that only the Son can pronounce, a word telling us that we have been created because we were chosen and adopted, according to the image of the only begotten Son, in order to participate forever in the divine life, holy and immaculate in love. This "agape," which was the very first love, forgotten and buried by the sin of Adam, is also the *last and final word* (the *eschatos logos* in Greek, from which we derive the word *eschatology*), the secret of creation that the Son pronounces on the cross and that traces out the limits of the world.

The fire of the burning bush is the fire of the Holy Spirit, the baptism of fire in which the Son of Man has come in order to baptize creation. "I came to bring fire to the earth, and how I wish it were already kindled" (Luke 12:49). This mystery involves man, since he himself is the vector of creation, being in the material world the only creature to be adopted. God created all the other beings using the imperative tense, whereas for man alone he employed the tense of love, a tense that does not exist in our verbal conjugations but that is the tense of the love of the Trinity for us, something that we refer to as the "divine counsel." It is in this kindhearted design of God, a design that is infinitely more than an order but is instead a mystery of grace: it is here that we can discover the origin of creation, at the very heart of the dialogue of the persons of the Trinity. If we want to assess the true value of creation, we must do so by referring to the measure of love. Our heart is the only meter capable of measuring love. And so we are the bearers of the purpose of creation because we are the bearers of its measure of love. But it is not a meter established in advance, regulated once and for all by some cosmic necessity. Instead it is an expandable meter, the pure communication of a gift, functioning in a manner similar to the heart at the center of the body.

CHAPTER TWO

The Humanity of God

At the very center of God's heart resides a mystery of grace, a "mad" and passionate love for man, a love "even unto folly." This already appears in the Old Testament. At certain moments, the veil is lifted and the visionary is able to gaze into the depths of God's glory. Such was the case for the prophet Ezekiel, who describes his experience in this way: "And above the dome over their heads there was something like a throne, in appearance like sapphire; and seated above the likeness of a throne was something that seemed like a human form" (Ezek. 1:26). This verse is a response to Genesis 1:28, where it is stated that man was created in the image of God. If man is in the image of God, that implies that man's image is also in God. In this text of Ezekiel, and notwithstanding the entire context of the Old Testament with its strict prohibition of idolatry, we witness the appearance of what a Protestant theologian of the twentieth century called the "humanity of God."

The mystery of the will of God, the secret of the liberty of his love, is man, such as the Lord wanted him, as the goal of his creation. This human form is also seen by the prophet Daniel, but this time it appears as mysteriously distinct from the Father. For Ezekiel, it was the vision of God himself, the One whose name is above every name; to this prophet, the splendor of the Lord's glory was manifested in the form of the man whom God had created and with whom he had established a covenant. For Daniel, at a more advanced stage of the Old Testament revelation, that same human form in God appears as a mysterious personage, a character who is distinct from the Ancient of Days, the Eternal Father: "As I watched in the night visions, I saw one like a human being coming with the clouds of heaven. And he came to the Ancient One and was presented before him. To him was given dominion and glory and kingship, that all peoples, nations, and languages should serve him. His dominion is an everlasting dominion that shall not pass away, and his kingship is one that shall never be destroyed" (Dan. 7:13–14).

Already in the Old Testament, someone in God is referred to as the Son of Man; it is someone who comes from God, who comes on the clouds of heaven, who comes from intimacy with the divine. This Son of Man has taken upon himself God's design for man. He carries the grace willed by God for men, the secret of creation, the secret that will cause creation to become the kingdom of God. "An everlasting kingdom was given unto him." No, God did not create an enormous piece of clockwork; he created a home to live in, a temple in which to take up his abode, a kingdom of which he will be the kindhearted, benevolent king. We know that the revelation of God the creator, as given to Moses in Exodus, is intimately related to the mystery of the covenant: "Thus you shall say to the Israelites, 'I Am' has sent me to you" (Exod. 3:14).

At the very moment when God reveals himself as the creator, he also reveals himself as the one who takes care of men, as the one who dearly values men. In a striking Old Testament formula, he declares, "One who touches you touches the apple of my eye" (Zech. 2:8). If God is that vulnerable in man, it is because he has placed him in the same relationship that he has with his only begotten Son. Therefore anyone who harms man "harms" God in that paternal-filial love from the heart of which he has resolved to give his grace to all those whom he has adopted as his children.

Before the ages, the Son of God was clothed by the Father with the blessing of the Spirit for men. Even before taking on our flesh in the Incarnation by being born of Mary, he put on the Father's love for us, because the Father loved us and chose us in him. From the very beginning, he became God's anointed, the Messiah or Christ (words that in Hebrew and Greek mean "anointed one"); it is he who clothed himself in the grace that is destined for us. Henceforth, as soon as man makes his appearance, he already belongs to Christ, and Christ, the only begotten Son, is linked to the destiny of the men who have been adopted in him. Paul says in the Second Epistle to Timothy, "God saved us and called us with a holy calling, not according to our works but according to his own purpose and his grace. This grace was given to us in Christ Jesus before the ages began, but it has now been revealed through the appearing of our Savior Christ Jesus" (2 Tim. 1:9–10). The grace of God's purpose for us belongs to us even before we are created; it has been promised to us, and it belongs to us in Christ, that is, in the Son inasmuch as he clothed himself with our vocation to be adoptive children of God. It is he who is ready to be the ultimate sponsor of our destiny, the guarantor of our vocation; it is ultimately he who must pay with his person if ever we fail to respond to the vocation that the Father has given to us.

The Secret of Being

The creative will of God is not a will that subjects man to any rigorously predetermined program. On the contrary, it is the love of a parent who arouses, assumes, and sustains the adventures of the liberty of his children; this liberty ought to express in the creature the rays of the grace that flows from the uncreated love of the divine persons of the Trinity and from their mutual gift. This mystery that presided over creation remains hidden if we attempt to understand the order of the world only from within. Paul explains this to the Corinthians, asking rhetorically, "Has God not made foolish the wisdom of the world?" (1 Cor. 1:19–20); we find here an echo of the main theme of the book of Ecclesiastes mentioned earlier. Worldly wisdom teaches many things that are true. Paul does not claim that it is false wisdom but affirms that it is folly—folly, in the sense of someone who would search desperately in a room for something that is not there. The wisdom of the world is looking for something that is actually a mystery of fire in the heart of being. This mystery of fire is a secret love that can only be received from the One who loves; it is the mystery of the will of someone who, in his sovereign liberty, enters into a relationship or covenant with man and reveals himself to him. Paul therefore appeals to another type of wisdom: "We speak God's wisdom, secret and hidden." This wisdom can only be revealed in a personal relationship, a wisdom "which God decreed before the ages for our glory." "None of the rulers of this age understood this," for it is something that "no eye has seen, nor ear heard, nor the human heart conceived, what God has prepared for those love him" (1 Cor. 2:7–9).

This wisdom is not a principle that one can deduce from the immanence of the world by studying the entrails of the cosmos. Saint John indicates to us that this principle is a Word. He opens his gospel by saying, "In the beginning was the Word" (John 1:1); this expression "in the beginning" echoes the opening phrase of Genesis: "In the beginning when God created the heavens and the earth" (Gen. 1:1). That which is "in the beginning" is thus not an element of this world. It is a Word that is addressed to someone, a living relationship; this is not wisdom in the form of the Buddha entirely plunged into in his own inner illumination but wisdom as it appears in Rublev's icon of the Trinity, where it is revealed as Word and breath, movement, communication, dialogue, and love. "In the beginning was the Word, and the Word was with God," propelled into the intimate "heart" (cf. John 1:18) of God, "and the Word was God. . . . All things came into being through him [in this circular movement in the most intimate "heart" or bosom of God], and without him [i.e., without this Word in the bosom of the Father] not one thing came into being" (John 1:1–3).

Already the Old Testament had reinterpreted the cosmic wisdom in which the peoples of antiquity sought the main principle of the world, the explanation of its order and perfection. The Bible had profoundly altered the themes related to the order and the wisdom of the world. In Proverbs 8:22–31, creative wisdom is seen as a mysterious figure who plays before God and who delights in finding her joy with the children of men. So in the place where we would have expected to find a majestic impassivity at the top of the pyramid of beings, we enter instead into a whirlwind. It is the world's heart, a heart of the world that does not belong to the world but is situated at the source of the world; before the world existed, this heart already was, and in it, everything was created.

The Passage of the Living God

We can now understand why the world, precisely in all that it has that is imperfect and transitory, in all its constantly changing historical and dramatic aspects, is a road to the discovery of its filiation; it bears within itself the unmistakable trace of that circular movement, the trace of that original gap in which it was created. It was not created in order to achieve, in a kind of perfectly spherical form, its own measure and its own internal order; it was created in a momentum, in a powerful impulse that traverses it and gives it its very being. For it was created through the Word. The world knows neither where this Word comes from nor where it is going, just as it does not know the comings and goings of the Spirit who carries the Word. We sense that something passes through the world, through history, through our lives, and yet we know neither its origin nor its end. How could we know without ourselves running through the trajectory that goes from the beginning to the end, without being swept away by that Word who runs his race like a bridegroom coming forth from his nuptial chamber, and who passes through all of creation from end to end? How do we enter into this wisdom which is the mystery of love, without entering into the movement or rhythm of love? How can we follow the road of this wisdom without giving our lives? For that indeed, in the final analysis, is the question.

Our world bears the traces of a passage. And although, by our sin, we have transformed this passage into a way of the cross, this world's vocation remains that of being a pilgrim route. If the world is changeable and nomadic in its being, how can we learn the first and last word without entering ourselves into the rhythm of its movement and traveling with it unto the end? That is why, in the middle of the night of the world, according to a passage from the book of Wisdom (18:14–15), when sin had rendered the creation's course completely opaque and incomprehensible, the eternal wisdom, the living Word of the invisible God, leaped down in order to visit us. It should be noted that the verb *to leap* is a verb that the Bible applies to wisdom. Wisdom leaped from the throne of God and came down to earth, bringing to mankind the revelation of God's design for us. Wisdom came to show us, in a flesh like our own, that we should not be afraid to enter into the crossing, into the Pascha or Passover; creation also experiences a passage or Passover, but it does not pass away in vain, for love is the secret of its passing. God has come to accomplish our passage together with us. It is a bit like mountain climbing: if a beginner is afraid to go over a difficult mountain pass, the experienced guide who has gone ahead leaps back across the chasm in order to pass over a second time with the beginner.

"For us men and for our salvation he came down from heaven," says the creed. It was necessary that the very same One who carried the secret of our origin and our end cross with us the most mysterious of all thresholds, the threshold that remained closed to us, as if by an impenetrable curtain: the threshold of life and death. "To God, the Lord, belongs escape from death" (Ps. 68:20); the final outcome of the mystery of our frailty and our passing belongs to you, O Lord. You alone, who are the living Word of the Father, can read through our story right to the end and show us that it is nothing more than an apprenticeship for the eternal Passover that will have no end: the one that goes from the Son to the Father in the Holy Spirit, and which is called love. This love, as Saint Paul tells us, "will always abide[;] . . . it will not end," even if everything else does pass away. Through love we enter into eternity, which is not a permanence of immobility but the infinite incandescence of the fire, which in the Trinity is the reciprocal gift of the divine persons in the heart of He Who Is; this fire is the passing of the Father into the Son and the Son into the Father; this fire is called the Holy Spirit.

And thus the One through whom all things were made, the One who bore the secret of our being, has "bowed the heavens, and came down" (Ps. 18:9); that is to say, he has henceforth introduced the passage of the life of the Trinity into the passage of our world; the joining together of these two passages is what we call the Passover. Henceforth, for us, all the elements of incompleteness and imperfection in this world, which ravage us and tear us away from ourselves, all that which apparently leads us off course and disperses us is, in fact, that which builds our eternal home in God. Through this apparent uprooting and this apparent dislocation, caused by the transient order of the world, our eternal home in heaven is constructed. Our earthly home is falling into ruin, but at the same moment, God, with the broken bits and pieces of our earthly mosaic, is preparing the heavenly Jerusalem. Heaven has come down on earth ever since the Son of man engaged himself in the race of life and death, in order to bring us into his eternal passage toward the Father.

The Son, the Firstborn of All Creation

To deepen our understanding of the role of the Son in creation, we can refer to a page in the Epistle to the Hebrews: "In these last days he has spoken to us by a son, whom he appointed heir of all things, through whom he also created the worlds" (Heb. 1:2–4). Thus God did not create the world for itself, simply in order to create something. God did not have any need to create. We say that it is by grace and out of love that he created. He gave the world a purpose, a goal, an orientation that surpasses it. This appears in the theme of the heritage that I have already mentioned: the world is not, for the Bible, a kind of entity placed into existence by God in the beginning, without purpose or meaning; it is an inheritance. We find ourselves here in a family context: God wants to give man that which he creates. In the book of Genesis (Gen. 2:19–20), God gives man dominion over the world; he brings before Adam all the other living creatures to see what name he will give them: man is thus established as the heir of creation. But in adopting man as his son and making him his heir, God introduces him by grace into the same place occupied by the Son in himself. It is therefore in the Son and for the Son that the Father conceives this loving design from which he will produce the creation; and man is the heir of creation because he is called, as Paul says, to reproduce the image of the Son: "We know that all things work together for good for those who love God, who are called according to his purpose. For those whom he foreknew he also predestined to be conformed to the image of his Son, in order that he might be the firstborn within a large family" (Rom. 8:28–29).

The creation is perceived as being enveloped in the mystery of grace, given by God to men. God includes men through the grace of adoption, in the person of his Son, and he confides them all to this Son, whose image he calls them to reproduce. As Jesus says in John's gospel, "The Father loves the Son and has placed all things in his hands" (John 3:35). The creation, by its finality of grace, is situated in the relation of the Father to the Son; its secret will therefore be contained in the mystery of the Son. As Saint Paul says, "[Christ] is the image of the invisible God, the firstborn of all creation; for in him all things in heaven and on earth were created. . . . [A]ll things have been created through him and for him. He himself is before all things, and in him all things hold together" (Col. 1:15–17).

This does not mean that the Son alone gives being to the creation: it is inseparably that the three persons, the Father, the Son, and the Holy Spirit, create. But the adoption of man in the Son is the purpose of creation, its orientation. And it is this orientation of creation that confers on it its form. We do not clearly see this in the current state of creation, because the journey that this creation must follow in the design of God has not yet yielded its final word. Its last word is precisely this reference to the Son. The Son, as the image of the Father, must be for man, who by his liberty is the vector of creation, the place where creation finds its definitive destination, which is the purpose for which it exists. The creation presents itself as the legacy of the Son, or, in other words, as the kingdom of which he is the Lord.

The world is not simply the "vast expanse" that Descartes considered it to be, but rather a mystery of an order that can only reach its ultimate goal in the grace of a filial relationship to the Father, a relationship of which the Son is the eternal archetype in God himself. The Son reveals this relation by giving man the ability to discover creation as an inheritance given to him by the Father. It is in virtue of the creative act of God that the creation exists, but its head is the Son, because "in him all things hold together" (Col. 1:17); it is linked with him by a relationship of grace that he gives to it from his own personal relation with the Father.

The Trinitarian Dialogue of Creation

At the root of creation is hidden a mystery of liberty; not only the creative and sovereign liberty of God in regard to his work, but also the intra-Trinitarian mystery of love among the three persons of the Trinity. It was in a dialogue of love, a mystery of mutual consent, that the supremely free decision to create was taken. In the unique divine will to create the world, each person plays his own proper, eternal role: the Father is the source, the Son is the response to this love, and the Holy Spirit is its communication.

In light of this we can clarify the mysterious passage of the Apocalypse, where Christ says: "[I am] the Amen, the faithful and true witness, the origin of God's creation" (Rev. 3:14). This "Amen" that is the origin or first cause can only be an Amen that is pronounced within God himself.

Because the Father assigned adoption as the meaning of creation and because he wanted man to come back to him as the bearer of this creation, it was necessary that the person in God who is the eternal image of sonship, the only begotten Son, pronounce his "Amen" in order to be the faithful and true witness of the Father's work and to be, in other words, the guarantor who would not flee if man ever happened to fail in his task. And thus there exists a last resort, in the very heart of God, an ultimate support for creation. It is the Son who says "Amen" to the work of the Father. This work is, of course, also his, inseparably; but like everything in the Trinity, its source is in the Father.

It is the same in the following passage of the Second Epistle to the Corinthians: "The Son of God, Jesus Christ[,] . . . was not 'Yes and No'; but in him it is always 'Yes.' For in him every one of God's promises is a 'Yes.' For this reason it is through him that we say the 'Amen,' to the glory of God" (2 Cor. 1:19–20). Our entire creation, all that we are, was enveloped at its very source in God, in his creative plan, by this Amen of the Son who thus became the firstborn of all creation, our elder brother. This does not mean that the Son of God was created first, as a creature before the others. It means instead that in the creative design or plan he assumed the role of the elder brother, of the one who would respond on behalf of all the others, in any and all events. It is in this sense that he is the mainstay of our vocation; from the first moment of creation, we belonged to him in grace.

God, as Saint Paul says, has sealed a mystery of marriage between humanity and his Son, and this occurred even before the foundation of the world. The Son is our Amen to the Father from before the foundation of the world, at the very source of the creative plan, from all eternity. At all events, humanity, carrying the mystery of creation and growing in God's love through grace, needed to go forth and encounter "the One who was to come" toward it. The eternal Son, who carries in God the archetype of what men should be with regard to the Father who chose them as his adopted sons, had to manifest himself in one way or another to this humanity that was adopted in him. How would humanity have been able to discover the Father's face, and how would man have attained the fullness of his filial relationship, a relationship to which he was called from the moment of his creation, if the Son had not appeared to him? Already from the beginning, God spoke to Adam, and this solicitude of God for man, this Word that he addressed to him, the breath that he infused into his nostrils, already indicated the beginning of a manifestation of the Father in his Son and in his Holy Spirit. Using a mysterious formula, Paul says that Adam was "a type of the one who was to come" (Rom. 5:14), that is, of the second Adam, the man who was to come. Adam was the first draft of humanity. He came out of the hands of God and was called to the grace of sonship. But how could this humanity utter its last word to God before its final status was revealed to it? And who had the secret of this final status if not the One who, in God, and from all eternity, is the only begotten Son?

Genesis seems to give us a glimpse of this mysterious presence of the Son at the origins of humanity, in the form of the Tree of Life that was to have given immortality (Gen. 2:9; 3:21). Because original sin has taken place, causing the path of human liberty to take a tragic course, we do not know and we may never know what might have been the extraordinary adventure of an unfallen Adam and his descendants journeying by the growth of their liberty under the influence of divine grace toward the ultimate encounter with the Son of God. We do not know either how this encounter would have been brought about. It would certainly not have involved an "incarnation," at least not in the sense of an "incarnation" in an individual human nature, since the Son would not have needed to take the place of man, who would not have damaged the image of God in himself. But, in one way or another, this mystery of the nuptials, this mystery of the "encounter" (which also happens to be the title under which the Eastern Church celebrates Christ's presentation and his entry into the Temple), would have been accomplished. In one way or another an unfallen humanity would have had to meet the One who, in God, is the bearer of the form of its predestination, the carrier of its secret.

How would man have been capable of saying the word "Father" in the full meaning of the term if the Son did not come to wed him in the Holy Spirit? However, it would not have been necessary that he come down from heaven in a single human nature at a precise moment in time. It is possible to imagine that he would have been reflected in the entire body of all humanity and that he would have been manifested in it more and more by deifying grace, as an image is reflected in a mirror. And thus he would have come to dwell in humanity through an invisible mission, in order to give man the ultimate form of glorification that would bring him to God forever.

Adam or the Prodigal Son

God wanted to give us the legacy of creation through his Son; he wanted us to discover that we are heirs in him. He wanted man's dominion over creation to expand progressively, as the image of sonship was gradually revealed in him. It is on the basis of his sonship, on the basis of his resemblance to the Son, that God wanted man to accomplish his role of ruling over the earth: "Let us make humankind in our image, according to our likeness; and let them have dominion . . . over every creeping thing that creeps upon the earth" (Gen. 1:26). Man's dominion over the earth is the consequence of his being in God's image. But man, jumping ahead of God's plan, resolved to seize the earth with his own hands, independently, and to take control of his own destiny. Here we have the mystery of original sin. Man attempted to procure for himself his ultimate happiness, without allowing himself to be led to the Son by the paternal pedagogy of God. He ignored the fact that he was only a first draft of the definitive Adam, the Adam of the future. He was still only the first sketch of the future Adam, that is, of the humanity for whom God was keeping in himself, the ultimate grace that was to be revealed in the Tree of Life as the fruit of immortality. In the place of this Tree of Life, man substituted a caricature, the Tree of the Knowledge of Good and Evil, involving a liberty that chooses itself and gives itself its own rules or standards, a liberty that claims to contain in itself the measure of its own ultimate good.

Let us return here to the parable of the prodigal son (Luke 15:12 ff.), which I have already characterized as an excellent explanation of original sin. The prodigal son, that is, every man in the footsteps of Adam, says to his father, "Father, give me the portion of the inheritance that is destined for me." *Portion*: the entire drama of sin resides in this one word, for God wanted to give everything. "Give me the portion of the inheritance that is destined for me": give me the world, your creation, since it is for me that you made it; leave me in peace, leave me *alone*, so that I can find there all that is good for me. The father actually wanted to give everything, but he wanted to give everything in communion; he wanted to share the heritage, not in the sense of cutting it up into portions or pieces, but in the sense of tasting and enjoying it together. This is indeed what happens later in the parable when the son returns, and they share everything together. From the start, the father wanted to be able to say to the prodigal son that which he later says to the faithful son: "My child, you are with me always, and all that is mine is yours." Jesus said these very same words to his Father: "All mine are yours, and yours are mine" (John 17:10).

But Adam chose to leave, so the Father gave him his portion of goods. The Father is bound by his love and by his respect for the liberty of his children. As soon as the prodigal son takes hold of his goods ("ripping them off," in the most literal sense of that colloquial expression), these, having now been detached from their creative source, become carriers of death. Here we have the fruit of death of the Tree of the Knowledge of Good and Evil; the tree that separates from the good and causes evil to be conceived. God, in contrast, does not see evil, not even as an idea. God wanted to give man the fruit of the Tree of Life; he wanted to share with him his eternal life; he wanted man to come into full possession of the world progressively, as he grew toward eternal life, without attempting to make himself, through the world, an absolute. In the knowledge of good and evil, the prodigal son squandered everything. When he finally came to realize that in this creation, full of the goodness of the Father, he had ruined everything, he said, "Father, I have sinned against heaven and against you; I am not worthy to be called your son." It is as if he said, "I did not understand you in your fatherly heart, I do not know that in your heart, as a Father, you wanted to share everything; you wanted me to inherit everything, after the manner of your Son who is the heir of all things, you wanted to make me the 'co-heir,' as Paul says, with the One to whom you have given everything, with the One to whom you have given your entire self, since he is God in you."

Now we can better understand the difference between the first Adam, our father in sin, and the last Adam, the second Adam, mentioned by Saint Paul, who is our elder brother for eternal life. Let us reread Philippians 2:6. I am proposing here a translation that, like any translation of so mysterious a text, is perhaps already an interpretation. I follow the text closely, word by word, in order to see if we can discover between the lines a reference to Adam: "Christ, existing in the form of God [as God's image], never sought to seize for himself equality with God." He was God's Son and his eternal image, but he never had the idea of acting as Adam did when he endeavored to take the inheritance into his own hands; Christ, since he is the only begotten Son, never considered equality with God as a prize that he should seize for himself. He always was, and forever is, with God, and all that the Father has also belongs to him. This is why he was able to act in a manner that is the direct opposite of Adam's larceny or "rip-off": he emptied himself completely, taking the form of a slave, taking the image of the Servant of God, in order to go in search of those who had fallen into slavery. In this passage of Philippians, we have a reference to the prophet Isaiah's Servant of God: "Taking the image of the servant and being made in the likeness of men." Being in the bosom of the Father, he was able to become the servant of the Father's plan. He manifested his love as the Son by divesting or emptying himself and becoming the Servant of God for our salvation. "For us men and for our salvation he came down from heaven," he who in heaven was the bearer of our secret, the secret of all creation, since "through him all things were made." He belonged to us so completely, he gave himself to us so entirely, he wanted so much for the creation to be completely taken up in his "Amen" to the Father, that he came after us, as one follows a lost sheep, even unto death.

The Coming of the Heir

One of Jesus's other parables speaks not only of the inheritance but also of the murder of the heir. I am thinking, of course, of the story of the murderous vineyard tenants in Matthew 21:33–44. A father had a vineyard that he entrusted to tenants. But instead of taking good care of it, they dilapidated the property. The father sent them servants, that is, the prophets, but the tenants mistreated them. The father then said, "I will send them my son, for they will respect my son; they will obey him." But seeing the son, the tenants said, "Here is the heir. Come, let us kill him, and his legacy will be ours." Here we have an interpretation that goes even further than that of the prodigal son. Not only is violence done to the father in order to obtain the inheritance; in addition, to seize the heritage in this way, the tenants resort to killing the heir who was guaranteeing the inheritance as a legacy of love. Here is the meaning of the parable: we can truly inherit this world (in other words, this creation), as the kingdom of God, as the inheritance of God in Christ, only by knowing and recognizing who the Father is, in the Son. When we chose to ignore, from the very beginning, who the Father is, we already condemned the Son to death. This is the meaning of the expression, "The Lamb slain from the foundation of the world" (Rev. 13:8 KJV). The Epistle to the Hebrews states this in an extremely mysterious and profound manner: "[Christ] is the mediator of a new covenant, so that those who are called may receive the promised eternal inheritance" (i.e., the legacy promised for ages in God), for "where a will is involved, the death of the one who made it must be established. For a will takes effect only at death, since it is not in force as long as the one who made it is alive" (Heb. 9:15–17). By the usurped possession and control that we wanted to exercise over creation ever since the original sin, we have, as the tenants in the vineyard parable, put to death the true heir; but it is his death, which he freely accepted in obedience to the Father, that will give us life and bring us back into the inheritance. For at the very moment when the Son is put to death, by "looking towards the one whom we have pierced," we discover the heart of the Father and the love he has for us. "God so loved the world that he gave his only Son" (John 3:16).

"He came down from heaven." The One who bears the ultimate meaning of creation and the mystery of its relationship to the Father had to come as the Servant in the livery of a slave, in order to reveal this to us, who had failed so miserably to recognize it. At one point in his gospel, Saint John makes the following solemn proclamation:

> Now before the festival of the Passover, Jesus knew that his hour had come to depart from this world and go to the Father. Having loved his own who were in the world, he loved them to the end. The devil had already put it into the heart of Judas son of Simon Iscariot to betray him. And during supper Jesus, knowing that the Father had given all things into his hands, and that he had come from God and was going to God, got up from the table, took off his outer robe, and tied a towel around himself. Then he poured water into a basin and began to wash the disciples' feet and to wipe them with the towel that was tied around him. (John 13:1–5)

What is striking is that to introduce the gesture of Christ as a servant, Saint John situates it in its Trinitarian dimension: knowing that he came from the Father, knowing that the Father had given all things into his hands. It is the heir of the householder who becomes the servant in order to teach the slaves what it means to be the Son. We would have had to learn this lesson anyway, even if there was no sin, but it would have happened in a much more transparent way, without pain or injury. But he loved us so intensely, he associated himself or identified himself with us to such a degree, to the point of having our name "engraved on the palms of his hands," as the prophet Isaiah said (Isa. 49:16 NIV), that he agreed to come and teach us in the role of the Servant.

We had become slaves, and in order to free the slaves, a slave was needed; to set the dead free, he needed to taste death; and to release those who were chained to the earth, it was necessary that he, the eternal wisdom of God, leap from his heavenly throne and come as one of us, as one among us. It was necessary that we be able to touch and see him in his individual form. And yet he was not simply one more individual; he was the Son by whom all things were made. Everything in him, in his flesh, in his humanity, was for us and for our salvation. That is why he can say that we are his body and, through this "individuated" body that he took upon himself as Jesus of Nazareth, he takes all of us, bearing our sins in his body on the tree. He is the head of all creation, our firstborn, having clothed himself with our destiny of grace before the ages. Therefore, by accomplishing that destiny at a precise moment in time, he saves the men and women of all ages and times. Although he joined us through the earthly existence of Jesus of Nazareth, this existence is nothing other than the manifestation in the flesh of the eternal Son in whom we were chosen before the foundation of the world. It is through him and for him that we were created. When we descended into the shadow of death, we drew him down from the heavens, we forced him, in his love, "to bow the heavens," as the psalmist says, "and descend" among us to reveal who God his Father really is, the Father who created us. He came to teach us how to become sons and heirs in him and with him.

Thus Paul can say, "All [things] belong to you, and you belong to Christ, and Christ belongs to God" (1 Cor. 3:22–23). Everything is yours, everything belongs to you, but only insofar as you belong to Christ, for the Father has confided you to him by adopting you as his sons. And you can only belong to the Son by entering into the relationship that he has with his Father, a relationship where nothing is shared by way of division but where everything is shared in communion. And thus we can understand how, even within the limits of a human life as ephemeral as our own, the Son of God revealed the secret of the eternal life that is promised to us as an inheritance. This secret consists not in seeking to eternally perpetuate that which we possess but rather in receiving creation as a gift from the Father, as a gateway to our future condition as adoptive children, a gateway that will take us into the eternal heritage of his glory.

CHAPTER THREE

The Innocence of the Father in Our Adoption

There is a formula originating in the New Testament that has become an expression of the faith of the church: God our Father created the world, and above all he created us, through his Son in the Spirit. Creation involves the Trinity, not separately for each person, but in a single creative act of the one and only God, with each divine person being present and active according to its irreducible originality. This is what is meant by the necessarily anthropomorphic term "the Trinitarian counsel." The term signifies that we were talked about and discussed in God, in the Trinity, even before our creation, from all eternity. Each divine person committed himself to this free act of love, to this kindhearted benevolent design, according to the original manner in which he exists eternally in God. The Father as source, the Son as image and Word, the Spirit as gift and breath. Each person in his originality was the subject of this single divine act that created us from nothing, out of an entirely free and purely gratuitous love.

Since it is done from the Father through the Son and in the Spirit, creation engages the Trinity especially with regard to man. In the book of

Genesis, as we have seen, it is only when man is mentioned that God speaks, using for the first time a mysterious plural: "Let *us* make humankind in *our* image, according to our likeness" (Gen. 1:26). With the creation of man, we have something entirely new, the reason for which everything else was created, that is, the image of God. Henceforth a creature will be a bearer, capable of reflecting, as if in a mirror, the most intimate life of the Trinity. For this reason, at this crucial moment, God speaks in the plural: "Let us make humankind"; he no longer gives orders but gives advice to himself, which is a very different thing. He does not say, "Let man come into existence," as he said, "Let there be light," "let the earth come into existence," "let the land bring forth plants"; instead, he says, "Let us make humankind." God says this to himself; the divine persons discuss it among themselves. The biblical phrase gives us this impression because this is indeed what is happening: "Let us make humankind in our image, according to our likeness."

What is the extra something involved in the creation of man? What is it that inspires God in creating man to already lift a corner of the veil that conceals his own Trinitarian mystery? It is precisely the fact that man is made according to the image of God. This will appear at the fullness of time, as the mystery of our adoption as sons, by the Father, in the Son, in the breath of the Spirit. We have been adopted; let us try to understand what this means. Before the world was, before we existed, there was a design of God, his "antecedent" will, the goal or purpose that finalizes his creation: to make us his adopted children, to dispose things in such a way that we are not external to him but adopted in the Son who is in the bosom of the Father, and so that in the Son, we are enveloped in the Spirit who proceeds from the Father and who rests in and "receives himself" in the only begotten Son.

Our adoption comes first in the divine intention that commands and presides over our creation. To understand this adoption, think of parents who want to have a child. They already desire the baby before conceiving it. This child is the object of their hearts' desire, and it already has a name; before coming into existence, it is already known in love. When the child is conceived, when its concrete existence begins, it is already preceded and enveloped by this desire that the parents had for it. The reason we have been created from nothing, the reason we exist, is that God wanted us as such. It is very important to remind ourselves of this in prayer, in difficult times, when we have the impression of not existing in anyone's eyes and when we seem to be touching the depths of our nothingness; it is precisely at that moment, from the very depths of this nothingness, that the word of adoption rings out, the word that drew us from nothingness in creating us.

A Choice That Causes Us to Exist

A saint who entered deeply into the mystery of God, Saint Catherine of Siena, suspended her entire contemplation on two key words of Christ. One day she asked him, "Lord, who am I for you?" The response that she received was overpowering, but it is something that we too must hear, sooner or later, in prayer. He said to her, "I am the One Who Is, and you are the one who is not." This devastating response was immediately accompanied by another phrase that gives another (complementary) perception: "If you exist, it is because I wanted you to be, since you are the one who is not, and yet you are; your creator and God is Love: the being that I give you comes from the Love that I Am." And thus Saint Catherine of Siena is able to say this astonishing sentence: "My nature is fire." We must not interpret this statement merely as an expression of the fiery nature of Saint Catherine's psychology. *Our* nature is fire: this is a fundamental truth of the faith that we can all apply to ourselves, because although by ourselves we are nothing, that which comes to us in virtue of the will of God who freely chose to adopt us is the Trinitarian fire of divine love that brought us out of this nothingness. As soon as we perceive this truth in all its radicalism, we are placed before the burning bush where God said to Moses, "I am the One Who Is"; this divine name implies that all the rest *is not*—everything else, by itself, does not exist. At the same time the bush burns without being consumed, because the fire of the divinity is what gives life and freshness to creation. Therefore we are made of fire; we are drawn out of our nothingness by the fire of this love of the Father who adopts us in the Son, a love that the Holy Spirit pours into our hearts and that is the source of our being. This is not primarily something sensitive or emotional; it accounts for the very fact that we exist, and this is a miracle, because by ourselves, we could not be, we could not exist.

We must not imagine our adoption by God as if it involved a choice by the Lord between creatures who had already come into existence in some unknown manner. In former times, when many children were given up to public assistance by people who renounced their paternity, the adoptive parents who presented themselves were required to choose this or that child as their own among all those who were there. It is not so with God; simply because for the Lord there are no unwanted children. This, by the way, is an atrocious expression that has become all too common today: we have become accustomed to speaking of "unwanted children," especially in regard to abortion. But no baby who has been conceived can be an "unwanted child" for God. Every child's conception goes through a process that is entirely human but also quite prodigious even from a purely biological point of view. But the mystery behind it lies in the fact that God has positively willed every human life that he allows to come into existence. Whatever may be the shortcomings due to sin, or simply to the weaknesses and failures of human parenthood, the fact remains that every child is desired by God.

Each one of us is thus chosen but not from a mass of already existing creatures from among whom we would be selected in a restrictive manner. It is not at all like in a basket of plums where some of the fruit is selected to make jam while the rest is left to itself and will inevitably spoil. No, our "election" coincides with our very existence; God chooses us precisely by pulling us out of nothingness. A choice of love, a loving gaze focused not on an already existing object but on that which does not yet exist (like parents who are about to conceive and who give the child a name even before its conception), such is the desire that God has had eternally and in which each and every one of us is unique. This is what causes us to exist; this is the mystery of our being. That is why our inner life of prayer and contemplation ought to consist simply in harmonizing our liberty, our love, our intelligence with this source of our being. To enter into prayer is nothing other than to enter into the truth of our being as Moses did when he approached the burning bush or as Saint Catherine of Siena did when she heard these two inseparable truths: "You are the one who is not (who does not exist) . . . and yet you are . . . for I have desired you out of love."

In this eternal design the Father wanted us, he saw us in his Son, and through the Spirit of love, he discerned us in our original uniqueness.

We were, each one of us, fashioned in God's heart when he fashioned us in the womb of our mother: "It was you who formed my inward parts; you knit me together in my mother's womb. I praise you, for I am fearfully and wonderfully made. Wonderful are your works; that I know very well. My frame was not hidden from you, when I was being made in secret, intricately woven in the depths of the earth" (Ps. 139:13–15).

Adopted Before the Foundation of the World

This adoption is revealed to us by Saint Paul especially in the hymn of the Epistle to the Ephesians: "Blessed be the God and Father of our Lord Jesus Christ, who has blessed us with every spiritual blessing in the heavenly places" (Eph. 1:3). Paul begins his letter with a prayer of blessing. He turns to the One about whom he is going to speak. He is going to speak about the blessing that God gives to his creatures, and he begins by blessing this God who is our Father. Paul "blesses" him for having "blessed" us in the heavenly places, that is, in his own most intimate mystery. The "heavenly places" represent the intimacy of God, his own presence to himself. This blessing that the Father has given us in the heavens in his Trinitarian mystery, this benediction through which he gives us the Spirit, is offered to us by him in Christ.

In verse 4, which follows immediately, we read: "just as he chose us in Christ before the foundation of the world." The blessing that comes from the Father, the blessing of the Spirit, elects or chooses us in Christ. That is to say, it chooses us in our most personal identity, which makes each one of us unique in God's eyes. We were elected, continues Paul, "to be holy and blameless before him in love." By this "election," God chooses us to make us creatures who will be completely sanctified in the presence of the Lord who is holy. This will be accomplished by sharing the love that constitutes God's very being. "He destined us for adoption as his children through Jesus Christ" (Eph. 1:5). We were predestined by him. This means that we exist by a choice that drew us out from nothingness and that orients us after the manner of an invitation or a calling. It is a bit like the blessings that the patriarchs gave each one of their children and through which they prophesied the grace of their particular vocations. God, in his predestination, assigns to us as our ultimate goal, the grace that will make us his adopted children.

Paul summarizes: "Such was the *kindhearted design* of his will" (Eph. 1:5).[1] This will of his is something totally free and gratuitous, because we are not God, we are not persons of the Trinity; we are called to enter into communion with the Trinity starting from nothing, having been taken from nothingness by an act totally free, totally gratuitous of our God and Father who discerned and called us from nonbeing to being. But he did not only call us to occupy the status of created beings; he also invites us to share the very life of God by participation in his love through grace. Such was *"the kindhearted design of his will* to the praise of his glorious grace" (Eph. 1:5–6).[2] We can truly give thanks and praise to the glory of God's grace, that is, in gratitude for this totally gratuitous love of God on our behalf. For in the magnitude of his kindhearted loving design, he has, from all eternity, discerned, chosen, and predestined us to be his children, sons in the Son, everlastingly. It is in the Son, inasmuch as he is the beloved of the Father, that the grace of adoption was predestined for us. This grace is a superabundance of love of the Spirit in which the Father gives himself to the Son and in which he envelops the Son.

Paul speaks of this same design in the Epistle to the Ephesians 3:9–11, where he says he is striving to "make plain *the administration or dispensation of the mystery*" (Eph. 3:9), or, to be even more faithful to the Greek expression, "*the mystery of the economy.*"[3] The "economy" is a dispensation that builds and organizes; the "economy" in Greek refers to the order of a household. God causes us to be his household, his dwelling place; the "economy" is the construction of the house of God. Now the dwelling of God with men constitutes the *mystery*, that is, his secret. This is not simply something that human thought cannot penetrate because it now lies above and beyond its reach. There are many "mysteries" in that sense: the "mysteries" that science does not yet know but will perhaps discover one day. These are not really mysteries; these are just things presently unknown. The true mystery is a secret of love that can only be revealed by the one who has conceived it. For example, the love of a young man for a young woman is, for the latter, a mystery until he declares himself and tells her about it; it is a mystery that comes from love and from liberty. We can only learn the secret of another person's liberty when that person opens up his heart to us. We have here a reality that is not only beyond our reach; instead we have a free-will decision that must be communicated to us. That is why, a little farther on, in the second part of the opening hymn from the Epistle to the Ephesians, Saint Paul speaks of the "*mystery of his will*": "He has made known to us the mystery of his will, *the kindhearted design which he has formulated in him [Christ] in advance*" (Eph. 1:9).[4]

A Wisdom That Is Innocent

The mystery of the economy is precisely the revelation of the secret of the divine will. On the level of his eternal purpose, when God looks at us in the desire of his love, he sees us only such as he wants us to be. This is one of the meanings of Saint Thomas Aquinas's phrase, "God does not have the idea of evil." In his eternal design, God does not foresee evil. Our faith must on no account ever lose sight of this absolute innocence of God with regard to evil. One cannot, of course, even imagine that God could be the author of evil. That goes without saying: one cannot be a Christian and believe that God may have wanted evil. And yet there is a stumbling block for the faith of most of our contemporaries. We know by heart a reproach that has been repeated to us at one time or another in our lives by unbelievers or people struggling under trials and tribulations: "If there was a God, there would not be all this evil in the world. . . . If God existed he would not allow it; or, if he really does exist, he must not be all that good after all and simply indifferent to our fate." Let us be honest with ourselves: Who among us can say that he has not encountered this stumbling block at one time or another in his life?

At the moment when he entered Gethsemane, just as this mystery was about to be unveiled, Christ said to the apostles, "Get up and pray that you may not come into the time of trial" (Luke 22:46). This particular trial involves precisely the danger of falling over the stumbling block of evil that stands between God and us. And the problem is not only due to the fact that we are subject to evil. The enemy, who is the first author of sin, Satan, the Accuser, actually plays a double game that consists in *accusing us and God simultaneously*. He accuses us of evil so that God will turn his face away from us and so that he will repent over his loving design for us. But Satan is also the accuser of God in the depths of our own conscience. He wants to prevent us from repenting. It is he who whispers into the innermost ear of our heart, saying that if we do wrong and then suffer the consequences, it is because, in the final analysis, God made us that way, and that therefore, ultimately, he only has himself to blame. After all, did we not come out of his hands badly shaped?

For this reason it is extremely important for our faith to confess that God, in resting his eyes upon us in his beloved Son, in his eternal gaze as the Father, cannot foresee evil, which he does not *anticipate*. How can one provide for that which *is not*, for that which not only *is not being* but also actually *destroys being*? Because that is what evil boils down to. God does not envisage or anticipate evil because it simply *is not*. Evil *is not*, and God is the One Who Is. He can only see us in the being that he gives us out of love, and in this gift, evil cannot be programmed in any way.

This fundamental certitude of our faith in a good God should be for us a very sure refuge during prayer in the midst of life's trials. In the first gaze that God casts upon us, the Lord meets us in the being that he gives us, and in this gaze, there is no consideration of our sin. To understand this we must contemplate the gaze of Jesus. In looking at us, Jesus never considers first our sin. In this his gaze is a truly divine one; it is the gaze of the Son that transmits to us the gaze of the Father. That which provokes conversion when Jesus looks upon us is the fact that he restores the look of blessing, which flows from the goodness of the Father and in which our sins are not anticipated or planned in any way.

We have difficulty imagining this, we who, starting from the time of original sin, are marked by the experience of evil. All human beings, with the exception of the Virgin Mary, and no matter how holy they may be, have a direct knowledge of evil. True, there are those who advance on the road to holiness to the point where, practically speaking, they no longer sin, like the saints who reach a high degree of perfection at the end of their lives. But even they know what evil is. They inevitably look at others and at themselves in a way that takes into account the fissure of evil as a parameter that cannot be ignored. Even when we are full of hope, even when we act according to the Spirit of God, all of us still anticipate and envisage the role of evil. The saints do this less and less. To them is given a supernatural prudence, the wisdom of those whose hearts are pure. And this wisdom enables them to take the role of evil less and less into account. But this is something that only happens at a very advanced stage in the spiritual life, thanks to the Holy Spirit's gift of counsel. And among them all, it never happens perfectly. What is absolutely incredible and unheard of in the gaze of Jesus, and in the way his gaze converted people, is that finally a gaze rested on them that was like living water, the water of the Spirit in which they were reborn, in which they were fully looked on in the exact way that the will of the Father perceives them in his design. Jesus did not have to tell the people he met what their sins were. He did not need to gaze on the evil that was in them.

The Gaze of Creative Love

One of the most moving encounters between Jesus and a sinner is that which takes place with the woman who was caught committing adultery in Saint John's gospel. There probably never was for a human being a more humiliating face-to-face encounter with God than that which this woman experienced as she was dragged before Jesus, before the holiness of the incarnate God. This woman cannot hide behind any arguments, nor can she invoke the help of anyone. She is as if identified with her sin. But something very mysterious occurs here: Jesus refuses to look at her. We are told that Christ stooped down and wrote on the ground with his finger. People often wonder what he was writing. But it is more likely that Jesus wrote on the ground in order to keep his eyes downcast so as not to look at the woman. During certain interviews, when we have the impression of standing before a wall of incomprehension, many of us have probably had the experience of taking a piece of paper and pen and scribbling drawings with downcast eyes. The real wall in front of which Jesus stood was not, however, this poor woman but the hard-heartedness of those who had dragged her before him. It is the devil who through these men brought her there to provoke a face-to-face encounter between God and evil, by confronting the Lord with this undeniable sin.

Satan puts all his efforts into trying to get God to conceive an idea of evil. Now this woman only represents evil because her sin is manifest and undeniable. But her accusers, and behind them the Accuser himself, are inhabited by evil in a much deeper way. Their sin, however, remains hidden. Jesus cannot cast his eyes on this woman, because God cannot look at her from the point of view of evil, as Satan wants him to do. For this reason Jesus addresses himself to the accusers without looking at them either, saying, "Let he who is without sin cast the first stone." But after they have all left, Jesus stands up, looks at the woman, and says, "Woman, has no one condemned you?" (It is as if he was saying, the Accuser is gone, and there is no longer anyone who is looking at you with an evil eye, with a look of evil accusation). The woman replies, "No one [has condemned me] O Lord." And Jesus then says, "Well then neither do I condemn you." In saying this, he looks at her. He does not say, "I know your sin and I forgive it." Jesus never spoke in this way. The first moment of the encounter with Jesus is always a time of healing and of *re-creation*. Only then does he add, "Your sins are forgiven, go and sin no more." But in the very first place there was healing, and this healing comes from the fact that Christ, as the creator that he is, sees and restores to existence the creature such as the Father willed it to be.

When Mary Magdalene enters the house of Simon the Pharisee with her vase of perfume, this same unique gaze of Jesus arouses in her a strong impulse of gratitude. Jesus had not yet spoken to her. He has not forgiven her anything. And yet she enters the house as someone who has already been forgiven; she is driven there by a rushing wave of gratitude, because she is aware of the contact with the One who has fully re-created her in her dignity. She knows immediately that everything has been restored to her. She does not need to hear Jesus pronounce a word. That is why Jesus is so deeply overwhelmed by her gesture. In silence, in the silence of Jesus, she understands who Jesus is, and that his gaze is the eternal gaze of the creator, who does not conceive evil, who does not foresee or anticipate it, and who does not introduce it into his designs as an element that he has to take into account.

This gaze will always be for us the most precious refuge when things get stormy. It is actually the sole driving force of our conversion, for it is the driving force of hope. Just when we say to God, "Lord, I know my transgressions and my sin is always before me," God replies, "My child, look at what you are for me." Like the father of the prodigal son, God does not keep an account of our sins. He puts us back in contact with the burning, incandescent love that makes us exist such as he wants us to be. And this is what overwhelms us and causes us to say, "Father, I am not worthy to be called your son."

We must constantly keep at the bottom of our heart, as its innermost cell or chamber, the gaze of God's mercy on his creatures. The purpose or design of God's heart, the loving gaze of the Father, the benediction of the Spirit that brings about our "election" in the Son, all this will always be situated first, as that which creates us, as that which comes first in relation to our response and to our sin. It will constitute an open source of living water flowing from God's heart for the purification of our sins. This source is the innocence of God, not only the innocence of kindheartedness due to the fact that God can in no way will evil, but a much more radical innocence according to which God in no way has any idea or concept of evil. This is why the icon of Fra Angelico invites us to contemplate, in Christ who is being insulted and cruelly mistreated, the face of God that is veiled with regard to evil. He is blind to evil because he *is* Being, and therefore he can in no way conceive nonbeing or the negation of being. This is the secret of his almighty power that is revealed through his apparent weakness.

Evil as Something Inconceivable for God

All this is beyond our categories, because evil is nothing other than a lack of being; and the lack of being is only possible in creatures for whom being is something that they "have" or possess and can therefore lose. But God *is* Being: "I am the One Who Is." He is the complete fullness of Being from which nothing can be removed. He does not have being as a possession; he *is* Being. It is possible to take away someone's possessions but not his being. For this reason God is at the same time infinitely poor, infinitely at the mercy of the evil that he cannot conceive. He is as innocent as a lamb who can be led to the slaughter without being able to open his mouth. He does not open his mouth, for the simple reason that he does not know what is going to happen to him. The wisdom of God, this wisdom that in the order of being is infinite in its resources and that created everything from the most distant galaxies to the infinitesimal entrails of matter, this wisdom that has created the human mind with all its wealth of feelings, this infinite wisdom is totally defenseless against evil and as if totally disarmed in relation to it. It is, as is written in the book of Wisdom, like a child playing before God and who finds its delight among the children of men. This wisdom is like a totally innocent child whom one can hit and who will be as amazed and stupefied as happens with certain child martyrs when their degenerate parents begin to beat and abuse them. Each year there are thousands of such children in the world, with parents who are insane or demonically possessed. These parents torture them, imprison them, or chain them in attics or in cellars. These unfortunate children are of course not exempt themselves from original sin. They too have a certain knowledge of evil, as well as some complicity with it. But nevertheless they suffer the hatred of their parents as something inconceivable, incomprehensible.

Indeed, when evil reaches a certain demonic degree, it becomes incomprehensible even for us sinners. In the case of God, the same thing is true for all forms of evil; even the least of them, the ones we are most used to, for example, our little daily laziness, our little selfishness, our bad moods, all the petty shortcomings that are for us, alas, like a "second nature," all these are inconceivable for God. In the face of evil, he is like a child who cannot say what it is. He can only know evil as a pure contradiction of his goodness, as a harsh and flat "no" that flouts his love, as a slap in the face, without any explanation. For us evil always has a certain explanation, except when it reaches its extreme, demonic limits. And thus our compassion is based on a comprehension of what evil is, because we too are capable of anything. But God cannot even imagine a possible complicity with evil. This is why his compassion differs totally from ours. He cannot enter our mental projections through which the idea of evil takes shape in our minds.

The Holiness of God, Our Ultimate Refuge

Some will find this innocence of God discouraging because he cannot understand our evil from within. He cannot even understand the very thing that, between us, serves as the motivating source of our mutual forgiveness.

We forgive each other because we know that we too are sinners; and so we often say, "Now it's your turn, but tomorrow it will be mine." There is always a little bargaining in our forgiveness: we forgive, hoping that we will be forgiven in turn, because we know that we are all involved in evil, whereas before God we are in the presence of the entirely Holy One.

We cannot, however, rely on any internal understanding of evil on God's part when we ask him for forgiveness. Where then can we take refuge? Saint Thomas Aquinas gives us the answer by the famous responsory *Media vita*, which was sung at the Dominican service of compline during Lent, a responsory that used to make him cry abundantly: "In the midst of life we are already at death's door; and from whom shall we seek help, if not from you, O Lord, even though your wrath is justly provoked by our sins: Holy God, Holy and Mighty One, Holy and Merciful Savior, abandon us not into the bitter grip of death." Even as we stand before the holiness of God who has no idea of sin, this holiness itself becomes our refuge. In the heart of God, in his design for us, we exist without any consideration of our sin. What we call God's forgiveness is actually the moment when the reality of what we are for the Lord enters into us, chasing out by its own fullness the evil that has been dwelling in us. In this way God in his holiness drives out the void of sin, closing the fissure, and reclaiming what is rightly his.

Contrary to what the devil tries to suggest, God's holiness, which cannot even conceive of evil, is far from being something that would separate us from him. On the contrary, it is precisely that which should cause us to confidently rush toward him. That is why in the Eastern liturgy, every time they sing, "Holy God, Holy Mighty One, Holy Immortal One," they immediately add, "Have mercy on us!" This compassion has nothing to do with what we call "pity." When we say "have mercy on us," we are not asking the Lord to consider with *pity* the *fissure* of nothingness where evil takes its source in us. Instead we are beseeching him to enable us to find ourselves once again within his creative gaze, since God our Father sees us in the heart of the Trinity with a loving gaze that chooses or "elects" us, adopting us from the very basis of the being that he gives us. And this divine gaze of his neither conceives nor anticipates evil.

CHAPTER FOUR

The Glorious Growth of the Liberty of the Sons of God

How is it possible to conceive what the course of human history would have been if man had been obedient to God's loving gaze, if he had allowed himself to be molded by the Spirit, if there had been no sin? Once again, it is the Epistle to the Ephesians that tells us what the main axis of God's design of adoption is and how God continues to want this design regardless of sin. "He made known to us the mystery of his will, the kindhearted design which he has formulated in him [Christ] in advance" (Eph. 1:9).[1] The mystery of his will is the kindhearted design that he formed in advance in the Son, regardless of what our response would be. This is the first desire that arises from God's heart, and it will be defined in verse 10: "This design which he set forth in him [in Christ] in advance in order to achieve it in *the dispensation, in the economy of the fullness of time.*"[2]

If there had been no sin, mankind would still have had to travel and grow in grace, and then, at the "fullness of time," that is, when the time was ripe, pass from its natural life to the divine life. Now, because of our sin, our salvation and our communion with the divine life have been taken up into the person of the Redeemer, the Son of God who has come in the flesh to accomplish our redemption and make our deification possible. But regardless of the Lord's recourse, because of our sin, to this particular way of accomplishing things, God's main purpose always remains the same: God did not create man in a totally achieved or completed state. He adopted man in his liberty and enabled him to become his child through grace while calling him to travel and grow through an economy of the fullness of time. This loving design of adoptive sonship had to be enacted in any event, whether or not there was sin. This economy or gradual process depended not on our sins, but simply on our nature. For a human creature whose nature is finite, becoming God is no small matter. Man has to travel a long way, and this is due first of all not to any resistance or refusal of his will, but simply to his limits as a creature. He must pass through various thresholds of growth, each one of which requires a trusting abandonment to God's will, through an entire economy of the fullness of time, which results in "the recapitulation in Christ of all things in heaven and on earth" (Eph. 1:10).[3] For, although we are adopted by God in his design, as his children in the Son, it is only through our ultimate identification with the Son that we can enter into the Trinitarian life. Even without sin, it would have been necessary, in one way or another, in a manner that completely escapes us, that the eternal Son recapitulate the grace of the adoptive children of the Father and that he be their head or chief. For he is the only begotten Son, the eldest among a multitude of brothers. As Saint Paul writes, "For those whom he foreknew he also predestined to be conformed to the image of his Son, in order that he might be the firstborn within a large family" (Rom. 8:28–29).

And thus an intimate communion between the adoption through grace, which has been given to us according to the form of the Son, and the Son himself, necessarily had to be established in the fullness of time. The Son is thus presented eternally as being the heir of creation. The term is very important: it means that the Son in any and all events had to take possession of creation, because the center of this creation is man, man who has always been desired by the Father in reference to the adoption of sonship in the only begotten Son. "Long ago God spoke to our ancestors in many and various ways by the prophets, but in these last days he has spoken to us by a Son, whom he appointed heir of all things, through whom he also created the worlds" (Heb. 1:1–2).

The Son *through whom* God created the world is the one *for whom* all things exist. All this must reach a recapitulation in him because everything was created in the Son according to a design for our adoption as sons. The theme of the heir is also found, as we have seen, in the parable of the wicked tenants. God first sends his servants, and finally he sends his Son; but the vineyard tenants say, "This is the heir! Come let us seize and kill him." Because he is the Son, he is also the heir (Matt. 21:38).

Entering into the Life of the Trinity

The design of the creator, his design of adoption, was meant to be completed in a humanity which, going from one threshold of grace to another, from one loving response to another, would eventually have completed its deifying entry into the life of the Trinity. The Genesis story speaks of the Tree of Life whose fruit is immortality. Man was meant to pass from this earthly life to the divine life, and this passage could only be achieved by a mystical marriage of humanity with the Son in whom God gives us the divine form of his grace. This passage, this entry into the Trinitarian life, requires that we become totally conformed according to grace, to that which the Son is as God according to nature. In the words of Saint Maximus the Confessor, in "divinization" we become through grace that which God is according to nature. More specifically, we become through grace that which the Son is by nature in relation to the Father, in the Spirit. It is given to us by the gratuitous love of God to enter into the same relation that the Son has in regard to the Father.

In whom could we have received this deifying grace if not in the Son himself, who is the only begotten Son, whereas we are only adoptive sons? Saint Paul alludes to this briefly in the Epistle to the Romans: "Adam is a type of the one who was to come" (Rom. 5:14). He speaks here in a positive sense. It is not by his sin that Adam prefigures the second Adam. It is as the first draft of sonship that Adam already foreshadows the fullness of divine sonship that was to come.

We obviously do not know how this accession would have come about in a world without sin. As we shall see, it certainly would not have supposed what we call the Incarnation, that is, the coming of the Son of God in an individual nature of the human species to take our place in a role where we would not have failed. The recapitulation would have been made by an *assumption* rather than by a *substitution*, since the Son would not have had to fill a place that had been abandoned by us. But it is still in Christ that we would have had to accomplish our ultimate passage into the bosom of the Father, because we could never have accomplished that passage unless the mystery of the Son was totally revealed to us. We can in no way imagine what form this ultimate communion of an unfallen humanity with the Son of God in the grace of adoption would have been. The fact is that, because of our sin, and for our salvation, this communion actually took the form of the redemptive Incarnation of the Son in an individual human nature. And thus he was "born of a woman, born under the law," in order to take away the curse of sin, death, and suffering and to accomplish for us what we had refused to do. We are here before something infinitely mysterious, indicating that the principal role of the Son in relation to us was to bring about our divinization and that, although it became in fact necessary for him to exercise this deifying role through his Incarnation as our Redeemer, the deification role itself was envisaged in any case by the design of the Father.

This deifying role of Christ is what Saint Paul calls the "mystery." He already speaks of this in the First Epistle to the Corinthians, when in contrast to the wisdom of the world he says that "we speak God's wisdom, secret and hidden, which God decreed before the ages for our glory. None of the rulers of this age understood this; for if they had, they would not have crucified the Lord of glory. But, as it is written, 'What no eye has seen, nor ear heard, nor the human heart conceived, what God has prepared for those who love him'" (1 Cor. 2:7–9).

That is the mystery: the culmination of our divinization through the Son, the Lord of glory. This mystery has in fact been manifested in Christ, and it is announced by the gospel, as Saint Paul says in the Epistle to the Romans: "Now to God who is able to strengthen you according to my gospel and the proclamation of Jesus Christ, according to the revelation of the mystery that was kept for long ages but is now disclosed, and through the prophetic writings is made known to all the Gentiles, according to the command of the eternal God" (Rom. 16:25–26).

The gospel, the preaching of Jesus Christ, is the revelation of the mystery that was wrapped in silence for long ages and is now revealed. Saint Paul refers to this same mystery in the Epistle to the Ephesians, calling it the "mystery of God's will" (Eph. 1:9). Likewise, in the Epistle to the Colossians, he writes, "according to God's commission that was given to me for you, to make the word of God fully known, the mystery that has been hidden throughout the ages and generations but has now been revealed to his saints" (Col. 1:25–26).

The Happy Redemption of an Unhappy Fault

Because of our sin, the redemptive Incarnation of the Son of God turned out to be the way through which the manifestation of the mystery constituting the "economy" of the fullness of time was accomplished. But, as I said, even if there had been no sin, this economy or dispensation would have at all events been accomplished, but it would have been enacted without a path of pain and tears for humanity and without the blood of our Lord Jesus Christ. Care must be taken not to misunderstand the formula "O felix culpa" from the Easter Vigil *Exsultet*—words so dear to Western spirituality but that remain a bit difficult to accept for Eastern Christians: "O happy fault that earned us so great and glorious a Redeemer." It would be quite wrong to believe that the fault, man's sin, merited for us the Son of God whom we would not otherwise have had without having sinned. This would amount to believing that evil, the evil that God does not conceive, would have somehow "upgraded" the ultimate goal assigned to us in God's design. It would probably be better to understand this text in the following manner: "O happy fault to which God responded by giving, in reparation, his Son as our Redeemer." God did not scrap, because of this fault, his original purpose, but he accomplished it by engaging as the active agent or instrument of the Redemption, his Son, in whom he had adopted us. But the Redemption does not "upgrade" God's design in its finality. As a manifestation of God's love, it is superior with regard to the means that it employs or engages,[4] but it is not superior in regard to its goal or end, which is none other than our adoption, willed by God from the beginning in his creative design.

When we think of the immense flood of misery and suffering caused by the so-called happy fault of original sin, when we consider the immense weight of sufferings borne by the Lord during his agony in the Garden of Olives, or when we think about the real possibility of damnation, a possibility that we cannot exclude because it derives from our liberty, we cannot sing the praises of this "happy fault" as if it were "thanks to it" that the Son was given to us. This would be an insult to the innocence of God, for it would boil down to presuming that God, in his first initiative, did not have a design that was generous enough to give us his Son. Pernicious ideas of this type can actually be seen as the distant origin of the rejection of God in modern atheism. If we imagine that God the Father, God the Trinity, did not give us the best in the first impulse of his loving plan, if we believe that our sin has somehow improved the goal that the Lord had in mind for us, we are in fact attributing to evil, to the evil that God does not conceive, a positive role, and this constitutes a real insult to the overwhelming goodness of the heart of the Father.

God's goodness in the redemptive Incarnation manifested itself in a new and extraordinary way, not in regard to the goal, but in regard to the instrument employed to achieve that goal. Of course, God could have saved us by a means other than by sending his Son in our flesh; but in sending him, he was only (in a certain sense) remaining faithful to his original design. He had promised that the Son would assemble us together in himself and "recapitulate" us; and now he gives the Son to us as our Redeemer. Indeed, after sin, the only way for us to be "recapitulated" is through the Redemption. God has remained faithful to his word; he has remained true to his original design, through flesh and blood and through the cross. The mystery remains the same: it is the mystery of the eternal design of adoption but which is now revealed through the history of our salvation.

Let us therefore always keep well in mind the fact that the Redemption does not bring to God's original design any additional advantage or bonus relating to our ultimate destiny. This must be true if only because the Redemption economy also presupposes the real possibility of damnation, which is something that we are required by the faith to believe. If damnation turns out to be an effective reality for some human beings, as is already the case for the demons, there will be something like "black holes" in the Mystical Body. In outer space astronomers have now discovered black holes. These are places where neutron stars have imploded on themselves and where matter has reached so dense a level of concentration that it is absolutely invisible, having become incapable of reflecting rays of any kind. These black holes are like chasms that absorb and destroy all the energy that reaches them, causing what is referred to as a "cosmic death" of matter.

It is terrible to imagine what the possibility of damnation represents for the entire Mystical Body of Christ. The damned would be like black holes where the torrent of the love of God and of all his creatures who in Christ have become the Lord's Mystical Body would flow into persons whose liberty or free will would immediately annihilate that love in them. Forever focused on themselves, these persons would extinguish all love, just as all light is extinguished in the black holes of the universe, which are no longer capable of emitting rays of energy.

If God is to wipe the tears from our eyes in the heavenly Jerusalem, these tears remain inseparable from the joy that comes from God's love when it is contemplated in and through the Redemption. The tears recall the great damage inflicted from the beginning, on the covenant between God and man. Although God has now committed himself in the person of his Son to save us, the original damage that has been repaired must always be looked upon as a major catastrophe. A crack in a glass can sparkle and shine in the sun as it catches the light, but this does not change the fact that the glass itself is cracked. Understanding this can help inspire and reinforce in us the gift of fear, not the fear of punishment, but the fear inspired by the delicacy of a love that knows that our relationship with God is as vulnerable as it is intense. The Lord's mercy assumes and takes charge of everything, but it is not with impunity that we sinners have spoiled the possibility of a virginal response to God's first proposal of love. It is true that the response of sinners to a love that redeems them is somehow rendered virginal again; but this response remains mingled with tears of regret over not having responded immediately to God's love but to have at first ignored and rejected it. The staretz Saint Silouan of Mount Athos has written some unforgettable pages about Adam's tears, and Masaccio has given us a moving painted representation of Adam and Eve leaving paradise in tears. At the spectacle of some of our brothers and sisters who are particularly weighed down and afflicted by evil, we begin to understand how tragic it was to have failed to respond to God's first manifestation of love with a love that was immediate and that did not need to be repaired.

The Imaginative Liberty to Accomplish Good

It would be insulting to God to think that he would have lacked imagination in love and that if there had been no sin human history would have been bland and uninteresting. Very often people are surprised when they are told that heaven is the supreme place of liberty. They sometimes respond with the following objection: in heaven there can be no liberty, because there it is impossible to sin. But making liberty consist in the ability to sin is a strange conception indeed. The possibility of sin is only the negative side, turned toward nothingness, of a created liberty that has not yet been fixed in its ultimate good, which is God; it is its shady side and not its bright side. Heaven is the place where liberty reigns supreme, the place where the pulse of love from the heart of God is diffused through all the liberties of the saints who are perfectly united to him. God speaks through his whole Mystical Body but with a variety of totally different accents: that is why God will grant certain things through the prayers of one saint and different things through the prayers of another. It is the same will of God, but it sprouts from a multitude of individual liberties through all the various charisms and personal graces that give each saint his or her unique face.

The history of humanity without sin would certainly have been a path in which man would have been called to continually outdo himself and therefore to walk in faith, because it is impossible to pass from the status of a creature to the state of total communion with the Trinity without leaping and ascending in faith from level to level. This is true not because of sin but because of the limitations of human nature. In order to progress, unfallen man would have had to trust the Lord. In the story of Genesis there is one threshold that was crossed successfully, and this is perhaps why it remains in humanity as a divine blessing that original sin did not abolish: namely, the gift of woman to man and man to woman in the formation of the married couple. After creating man, God presented to Adam one by one all the animals so that he could give each of them a name. In this way Adam exercised his dominion over the animals, but he did not recognize himself in any of them; he did not find in any of them that which he lacked and which was not "something" but "someone": a companion. Adam waited for God to fulfill this desire, and the Lord responded to his expectations. This story signifies that the mystery of the complementarity between man and woman in marriage and procreation is like the first human communion with the will of God in faith. Marriage and procreation constitute therefore an extraordinary form of cooperation between man and God, since through the union of a man and a woman God gives life to new creatures destined to live eternally as God's children.

We have here an extraordinary covenant made with Adam, and to which man opened himself from the very beginning. It can be seen as a first flowering of humanity in this initial discovery of conjugal love before original sin. It is like a foreshadowing of what might have been all the other thresholds that man could have crossed in faith, by opening himself through grace, to ever new spaces of liberty, by receiving himself from the hands of God through a gradual process or "economy" of education that would have stimulated his growth, until he reached the point where, in his humanity, the eternal face of the only Son of God was perfectly reflected. The Son would have thus wedded the entire human race by recapitulating it in the deifying grace of adoption. But this would have been achieved according to a modality that we do not know, since for us, because of our sin, it has been accomplished through the redemptive Incarnation in Jesus Christ.

All Things Recapitulated in Christ

In several passages of the New Testament it is stated that creation was made for Christ. We have been adopted in Jesus Christ, chosen in him "before the foundation of the world" (Eph. 1:4). "There is" only "one God, the Father, from whom are all things and for whom we exist, and one Lord, Jesus Christ, through whom are all things and through whom we exist" (1 Cor. 8:6). Here we see that Paul attributes our creation not only to the Word, but to the Word as the Christ. The One who was manifested as Jesus in the economy of the Redemption is shown to have been, as the Son of God, eternally designated in the Lord's design as the Christ or Messiah. Why is this? Because *Christ* means "the anointed one," "the one who receives anointing." But what is the anointing that is being spoken of here? It is none other than the blessing in the Spirit mentioned at the beginning of the Epistle to the Ephesians. This anointing is the gift of the Spirit; the Son is the "Christ," that is, the Anointed One, in the sense that the blessing of the Spirit that he carries is our adoption in Him; it is an extension through grace of that which he is by nature.

Even without sin, he would have recapitulated us by giving us the anointing of his sonship. "'The first man, Adam, became a living being'; the last Adam became a life-giving spirit. But it is not the spiritual that is first, but the physical, and then the spiritual. The first man was from the earth, a man of dust; the second man is from heaven" (1 Cor. 15:45–47).

The grace that was promised to us was an anointing of sonship, a blessing of the Spirit. The Son is the one who, from all eternity, carries in himself the kindhearted design of God as an anointing with the Spirit of adoption. "God sent his Son . . . so that we might receive adoption as children" (Gal. 4:4–5). He caused this adoption to be conferred on us in Jesus Christ as the Redeemer. But even if there had been no sin, the conferring of adoptive sonship was the "Christly" or "Messianic" role of the Son in the eternal design of our adoption by God the Father. From all eternity the Son belongs to us, or rather we belong to him. He himself is the Chosen One of God, that is, the One in whom we are chosen. It is a title that is given to him in the gospel: John the Baptist declared, "I saw the Spirit descending from heaven like a dove, and it remained on him. . . . And I myself have seen and have testified that this is the Son of God" (John 1:32–34). Of course this declaration must in the first place be understood of the historical Messiah. But, beyond that, there is the mysterious election in the Son "before the foundation of the world." This same title appears in Luke's account of the transfiguration: "This is my Son, my Chosen; listen to him!" (Luke 9:35). Here the link is very strong between the eternal sonship of Christ and our election of grace in him. He is the only begotten Son in whom we are destined to be sons by adoption.

Christ appears as the Son in whom God has placed his kindhearted design. From all eternity, the Son is the bearer of the mystery, that is, the loving design of God for men. This was already made clear when Jesus was born in Bethlehem. The angels sang, "Glory to God in the highest, and on earth peace to men who are the object of his loving design" (Luke 2:14).[5] That is exactly what the Greek text means. In many current liturgical translations it is rendered approximately by "peace to His people on earth, to the people whom He loves." In the past it was translated word for word as "peace to men of good will," but this tended to be misunderstood: the text is not referring directly to the goodwill of the men themselves but to the fact that men belong to the goodwill of God; they are the object of God's goodwill. This is what the angels declared when the Son, who is in himself (in person) the mystery of God's loving design, came in our flesh to bring the grace of adoptive sonship to men. Likewise in the gospel narratives of the baptism of Christ, the translations usually say: "This my Son, the beloved, with whom I am well pleased" (Matt. 3:17; Mark 1:11). But it is always the same Greek verb that is used and that means "in whom I have placed my loving design." Christ is the bearer of this kindhearted design. Likewise in the scene of the transfiguration, as it is mentioned in the Second Epistle of Saint Peter, we read, "This is my beloved Son in whom I placed my kindhearted design" (2 Pet. 1:17).[6]

The Son of God as the Spouse of Humanity

The Son, as the Christ who has been anointed in view of the eternal design of grace, is the bearer of the mystery of the divine will by which adoptive sonship in the Spirit is given to us. Because of sin, the Lord had to pass through our flesh and undergo death on the cross; but it is always the same eternal purpose that is accomplished by him. God, with a kind of obstinacy, the gentle obstinacy of innocence, accomplishes his eternal design by passing through evil but without taking this evil into account in the loving initiative of his antecedent will. However, by implementing with a blind love his loving design, he indwells the ground of our liberty, thus producing the economy of his "consequent will" in which God does take into account our free-will decisions. Thus when the only begotten

Son comes to wed our humanity after original sin, he finds no other entry into the bridal chamber other than his Incarnation and birth from the womb of the Virgin Mary and no other destiny than that of being put to death by sinners. The mystery of the bridegroom, however, would have been fulfilled at all events, with or without the occurrence of sin. The deepest mystery of the Son in his role as Christ consists in his being the spouse, the spouse who, by wedding us, brings us to God. In actual fact, he wedded humanity on the cross. Without sin he would have wedded mankind in a different way: humanity as a whole would probably have passed by a sort of "dormition," something like what the Virgin Mary went through, dying a different death from our own and passing in a last act of faith and love through an ultimate divestiture of herself, of her mortal life, in order to enter into the immortal life of deification.[7]

It is only with difficulty and hesitation, by stammering, as it were, that we can express anything about that which what could have happened but which did not occur because of our sin. We do, however, know what we cannot say. We must not say that God takes evil and sin into account in his creative design, in the loving initiative of his antecedent will. It must also not be said that the occurrence of evil and sin elevated the generosity of the heart of God the Father with regard to the end or goal that he intended for us from all eternity. To maintain any of this would be the equivalent of insulting the absolute innocence and the adoptive blessing of God the Father who is Love and nothing but Love.

CHAPTER FIVE

The Goodwill "Even unto Madness" of the Lamb of God

God's eternal design involved our adoption through grace according to the image of the only begotten Son who became the Christ or Anointed One (i.e., the head from which the anointing of the Spirit flows). But how did this design, even before the foundation of the world, assume the shape of the Lamb? This is indeed what is affirmed by a very mysterious expression from the First Epistle of Saint Peter: The Lamb "was destined before the foundation of the world" (1 Pet. 1:19b–20a). How is this possible if, as we have seen, God did not anticipate evil when he conceived his loving plan? If we consider what love is, even simple human love, how can we think that God would offer his love while taking evil into consideration? When we are in love with someone, even on a purely human level, we do not subordinate our love to the answer we expect to receive. Lovers always have a touch of madness about them, and they always tend to automatically assume that their love will be returned. (Indeed, this can often lead to comical misunderstandings.) The "madness" of love consists in its being pure initiative. Love characteristically has the innocence of a blind impulse, and for this reason, lovers sometimes are in danger of ending up "high and dry" as the common expression goes. But it is in the nature of love to be first, to take the initiative, and not to propose itself conditionally depending on the response. Of course the answer is expected, and this is true even in the case of God, but he offers his love to the liberty of his creatures and does not impose the response as some sort of preestablished program that would automatically determine everything in advance.

The Capacity to Sin as Inevitable but Sin Itself as Unpredictable

It is precisely the mystery of our liberty that causes the eternal design of God to take the form of the Lamb; the mystery of liberty with its peccability, with its ability to sin but not with sin as such, which is neither necessary nor inevitable. It is true that God took a risk in giving us liberty. Since he conceived a design of adoptive sonship, we needed to respond not as slaves but as sons, and this required that we be free. But liberty, for a creature that has only begun to grow in grace toward full communion with God, presupposes the possibility of sin. Since God did not want to cut short the road we needed to follow from our condition of creatures to himself, he accepted the vulnerability of his design from the beginning. But it was in no way necessary to his design that peccability (the capacity to sin) actually become sin. None of our sins are inevitable or "necessary" in themselves (even after original sin, although the latter has left in us a propensity toward sin and evil). And so there is even less reason to imagine that in the beginning, just because God was proposing his kindhearted design to small, fragile creatures, this fragility would necessarily and inevitably have ended up causing sin sooner or later.

So false a notion would in one stroke reduce to nothing in our minds the immense shock that sin really represents for God. It would amount to maintaining that God had already accepted the idea that, since he was proposing deification to poor humble creatures—something that in itself is a bit like folly or madness—he would have to resign himself to their sin as an inevitable result. We must not compare God's design to business enterprises where they foresee that some of their pipes will break and where they take these into account in advance when calculating their profits and losses. In our human projects we need to take into account all the things that are not going to work, and we resign ourselves to this in advance. We "make allowances" for all that can go wrong. God, however, does not work in this way. It is awesome to contemplate, but that is the way it is. We are completely baffled when we become aware of this absolute innocence of God who does not anticipate our sin and who does not take it into account in conceiving his design of love.

Because he created us free and because our liberty as creatures that have not yet been deified includes the possibility of sin, God took this risk upon himself from the beginning but only as a possibility. But sin itself was not taken into account in his creative design in terms of a predictable probability. Therefore sin is the most unpredictable of things, which directly opposes and contradicts God's design in the full force of the term. God cannot guard or ensure in advance his design against sin. That would involve for him having the idea of evil in the antecedent will of his initiative of love. He can only take charge of sin after the fact, once our freedom has committed it, that is, in its consequences. We ourselves cannot do much in advance against evil, except to remain anchored in the good. Excessively scrupulous people who are constantly trying to protect themselves against their flaws and faults are not really on the right path. The best morality is the one that gives us the desire and the flair for that which is good, and for the happiness that comes from goodness. This alone can enable us to forget the nightmare constituted by evil, a cancerous hallucination conjured up by our liberty but which in itself is nothing, having absolutely no consistency. It would be virtually impossible for us to count too much on the Lord to console us over the terrible nightmare of evil. He would like to arouse us from this pernicious dream so that awakening, we could find ourselves, like the child described in Psalm 130, tightly held against his heart, securely wrapped in his benevolent design in which he loves us without any anticipation of evil.

God's design is to eternally adopt us in the Son, that is, in Christ, who is the bearer of the grace with which we ourselves are to be anointed. And because this design does not in any way include evil, it takes the form of "the Lamb without defect or blemish. [Christ] was destined before the foundation of the world, but was revealed at the end of the ages for your sake" (1 Pet. 1:19–20). In this text Saint Peter applies to the Lamb the same expressions that Paul uses to describe the mystery of the loving design of our adoption, prior to the foundation of the world: "A mystery that has been hidden throughout the ages and generations but has now been revealed to his saints" (Col. 1:26). We have seen above that the title "Christ" can already be given to the Son of God in the eternal plan. Therefore we should not be surprised to find in the text of Saint Peter that "Christ was destined before the foundation of the world, but was revealed at the end of the ages for your sake." This "Christ" destined before the foundation of the world is the Son of God inasmuch as Saint Paul says that "those whom he foreknew he also predestined to be conformed to the image of his Son, in order that he might be the firstborn within a large family" (Rom. 8:29).

The Lamb, Blameless and Spotless before the Foundation of the World

But Saint Peter brings in a new element. For him, Christ who is destined before the foundation of the world takes on the figure of the Lamb: he is "the Lamb without defect or blemish." What does the expression the Lamb "destined before the foundation of the world" signify?

It should be noted first that the Lamb is "without defect or blemish." This is an allusion to the legal requirements concerning the paschal lamb: this animal had to be "blameless," that is, without any disease or defect due to some malformation; at the same time, it had to be spotless, that is, entirely white. The lambs who were brought by the Israelites to the Temple of Jerusalem had to be carefully examined by the Levites before the animals could be offered in sacrifice. This immolation of the paschal lambs took place on the day of preparation of Passover, which in the year of Christ's death seems to have occurred on Good Friday. According to Saint John, it took place at approximately the very hour when Jesus expired on the cross. This corresponded precisely to the time when they slaughtered the lambs that were to be eaten on Passover evening, that is, on Friday night. It seems that Jesus himself anticipated the celebration of the Jewish Passover meal with his apostles, precisely because the next day, Good Friday, he was to truly accomplish the Passover in himself. And thus it was at the very moment when the lambs were being slaughtered that the Lamb par excellence was slain. As Jesus expired on the cross, the priests who were sacrificing the lambs were singing Psalm 136 in praise of God's faithfulness, with the repeated refrain, "because his mercy is everlasting."

Now if we consider that Peter says that this blameless and spotless Lamb is Christ, discerned before the foundation of the world, then this Lamb is nothing other than the design of God's heart. In his account of the Passion, Saint John brings together two seemingly unrelated texts, the ritual prescription from the book of Exodus concerning the paschal lamb that was to be eaten on Passover night, and whose bones were not to be broken, and a text of the prophet Zechariah concerning a mysterious person who is "pierced." This latter text develops and deepens the theme of the Suffering Servant, who seems to be identified with God himself: "They shall look upon *me* whom they have pierced" (Zech. 12:10 KJV), says the Lord. There is a kind of assimilation here between the One "who is pierced," the Suffering Servant (Isa. 53:5), and God himself who will be pierced in him. Saint John saw that when Christ on the cross was already dead, they did not break his legs, as they did to the two thieves who were crucified alongside him and as was customary to do to those who were condemned to die on the cross, but that Jesus's side had been pierced with a spear. All this led the evangelist to make a connection between two seemingly very unrelated biblical texts. None of the Lord's bones had been broken, and therefore he is the Lamb — but as the Lamb he signifies the mystery of God's love, which can receive the most radical contradiction from sin.

If it was not permitted to break the bones of the Passover lamb (Exod. 12:9, 46) in order to eat the marrow and if Christ's bones were not broken (John 19:36), it is because the bones in the Jewish conception signify the skeleton, that which remains of someone's personal identity in his corpse, in his dead body. It took a very long time before the Jews came to admit a belief in the immortality of the soul. They had a very corporal way of understanding the hereafter. They believed that the final resurrection had to be accomplished from the actual remains of the bodies that had been buried in the earth. The bones and the skeleton appeared to be that which makes the connection between our present existence and our future risen existence. The bones were for them the concrete sign of that which does not perish in the person whom God preserves for eternal life (Ps. 34:20; 139:15–16). The breaking of someone's bones seemed to undermine that person's identity and his very soul.

Christ the Passover Lamb had none of his bones broken. For Saint John this manifests a definite connection with the resurrection and with the mystery of Christ's divinity. It is the Son of God in Christ who is pierced and penetrated right through to the heart, to the very center of his divine loving design, because indeed this design was conceived in the heart of God. "The thoughts of his heart [are] to all generations" (Ps. 33:11): this design springs from the heart of God, from his love and his liberty. The contradiction of evil violates this purely gratuitous love and wounds God in the heart of his freely chosen initiative. But precisely because God is injured in a pure design of grace, the evil cannot alter what we would call, in abstract language, the transcendence of the "Father of lights, with whom there is no variation or shadow due to change" (James 1:17). It seems that on this point Saint John perceives a distinction between, on the one hand, the two thieves who were executed and whose legs were broken and, on the other, Christ who on the cross had his heart pierced by the spear but whose bones were not broken. It is as if the most radical wound inflicted on the love of God necessarily had to go hand in hand with the immutability of his being: "When you have lifted up the Son of Man, then you will realize that I am he" (John 8:28).

By expressing the mystery of God's design through the figure of the Lamb, Saint Peter manifests the total innocence of God whose love is blameless and spotless, involving no compromise whatsoever with evil. In no way does God's love consider, take into account, bargain with, or compromise with that which we call evil. God has nothing to do with evil, whose sole origin is found in the liberty of men or angels when they say no to God.

The Growth of a Marian Type of Liberty

God, it is true, created us in our smallness, in our finitude, in our condition as creatures. But he created us by calling us to grow toward him, through his grace. He wanted our growth to take place through an entire economy where our liberty would be educated according to the pedagogy of love. This could only have been accomplished gradually and by having us pass over a series of thresholds, that is, by enabling us to undergo various types of death to ourselves, not death to any sin, since there would have been none in an unfallen world, but death to our limits as creatures. It would have been somewhat like the Virgin Mary, who was preserved through grace for all sin at conception but who had to grow in faith by following her Son. There are many things she perhaps did not understand but had to accept. If it were possible for us to compare Mary as the young girl of the Annunciation with the mature woman she became, the woman who accompanied the church after Pentecost together with Saint John the Evangelist, and then probably lived for a long time in Ephesus, outside of Israel, in pagan territory, we would see the tremendous amount of growth that took place within her. Mary traveled a long road, which was not really a "road of conversion" since she did not need to convert from sin, having been radically saved by "prevenient" grace, that is, by the grace that preceded her from the very first moment when she came into existence. But she had to go through many thresholds of self-abandonment with respect to her natural desires, thresholds of dying to her own limits, right up until her final "dormition" which involved abandoning her earthly condition in order to enter, through the passover of Christ, into the heavenly condition of the glorious Resurrection. There is in this path followed by the Virgin Mary perhaps a reflection of what the path that our liberties might have been if man had not sinned, a path involving all the growth necessary before being able to eat the fruit of immortality from the Tree of Life but a journey that, as Mary's life itinerary shows, did not inevitably have to involve man's eating of the bitter fruit of the Tree of the Knowledge of Good and Evil.

There Is No Pedagogy of Evil

In creating us, God willed our finitude, our smallness, and the journey of growth in deifying grace that our liberty was called to follow. All this in no way tarnishes the mystery of the Lamb who is blameless and without spot, since there is nothing in this design that necessarily required a passage through sin. To admit the contrary would be to introduce into our minds, as I warned earlier, a suspicion that poisons all modern thought, the image of a sort of sadistic God who would have created us in such a way that, no matter what, we would necessarily have had to go through "this valley of tears." Worse yet, to this suspicion of sadism is added that of masochism when we imagine that God not only conceived the tragic scenario that is that of the entire human race, but that he also doubled it with a masochistic scenario in which he involves himself in the person of his Son, whom he takes pleasure in seeing put to death on the cross. So atrocious a suspicion is bound to insinuate itself into our minds if we accept that God, in his benevolent loving design for us, actually wanted sin and all its consequences, if only indirectly, as a necessary road for us to take, as a means for educating us. On the contrary, we must reject this false idea and fully accept instead that we are, along with the fallen angels, the sole and exclusive authors of sin. We must not allow the holy innocence of our God to be in any way compromised by this work of evil, which comes from us alone as creatures. The Lamb must be free of even the shadow of a spot or of any possible reproach that we could address against the loving innocence of the Father who can only want good things for his children.

On this important point, we very much need, in our prayer, to let our encounter with the Father's entirely loving heart purify our imagination, which relies on our experience of human fatherhood and motherhood as the basis for its knowledge of God. Whatever may have been the holiness of our parents, and very often it was very great indeed, they themselves were nevertheless poor sinners. The face of their human parenthood on which we tend to decipher divine fatherhood is wounded by our own sin and theirs. Therefore, we often project onto divine paternity suspicions that come from poorly healed wounds of the filial relationship we have had with our own parents.

Love without Exclusion

The eternal design manifests that, in the Lamb, God has a universal will of love for all mankind and from which he does not want to exclude any one of his children. No one is rejected (and to imagine the contrary would be an intolerable blasphemy) or even loved with a certain coldness, as we see in certain families where parents do not put their entire heart into loving one or the other of their children. Alas, to imagine something like this is to project onto the mystery of the divine fatherhood the caricature of sin. In the Lamb who is blameless and spotless, there is a love for every man that goes right "to the end" (John 13:1).

We must tirelessly reiterate that there is not a single creature that has or will come into existence; there has never been and never will be a single being of our human species, starting with the most primitive men (*Homo sapiens*) at the dawn of humanity to the men of the civilizations at the end of time, who is not loved by God as his child in his beloved Son. We must firmly adhere to the very clear and unambiguous affirmations of Holy Scripture in order to thwart any suspicion that might creep into our hearts. And indeed, formidable suspicions have found their way into tradition, sometimes due to spiritual authors and theologians, especially in the West, when discussing the theme of predestination. These authors believed that they had found in scripture the affirmation that some people are not predestined to divine sonship in the design of God's antecedent will. And so they assumed that there might be some persons who are simply created by God but toward whom he might have a sort of supreme indifference, leaving them to themselves, that is, to their doom.

As a defense against such horrible rantings, we must continually keep before our eyes the bright words of Saint Paul: God our Savior "desires everyone to be saved and come to the knowledge of the truth" (1 Tim. 2:4). We find the same thing in several phrases pronounced by Our Lord Jesus himself: "This is the will of him who sent me, that I should lose nothing of all that he has given me, but raise it up at the last day" (John 6:39). In the same gospel of Saint John, at the end of Jesus's discourse on the Good Shepherd, we read, "My sheep hear my voice. I know them, and they follow me. I give them eternal life, and they will never perish. No one will snatch them out of my hand. What my Father has given me is greater than all else, and no one can snatch it out of the Father's hand" (John 10:28–29).

The Father has given us from all eternity to his Son, by adopting us as his children. All men without exception are in the hand of the Father, and this hand is Christ himself, and nothing except we ourselves can separate us from the hand of the Father. That is the central aspect of the mystery of the Lamb: the absolute innocence of a God who unto the end loves each one of us with a love that is without reproach and without tarnish. As Jesus said at the end of the parable of the lost sheep, "It is not the will of your Father in heaven that one of these little ones should be lost" (Matt. 18:14).

The Father's will is that none of these little ones should perish. And this will is not a mere wish; it is the eternal purpose of God. It is a will for which God is prepared to make sacrifices if necessary. He will pursue every creature with his love to the end. The justice that God owes to himself in the design that he has conceived is to never stop loving those whom he has created. Any cessation of love of God for one of his creatures would be a stain, a reproach on the robe of the Lamb. God owes it to himself to be pure love and nothing but love, loving, as it is said of Jesus, "to the end" each of his creatures. Here precisely is the form of the benevolent loving design of God for all mankind, foreknown before the foundation of the world, as the form of the Lamb.

The Creator's Design of Grace

In the New Testament, this design that precedes the creation of the world appears as a mystery of grace. We are used to thinking of grace as being that which follows nature; we think of grace as the elevation that God gives so that we can reach him after he has created us. But we forget that our creation itself is a mystery of grace because it is oriented to a finality that is the design of our adoption. Even before the creation of the world there is the gratuitous grace of the love of God for us, whom he creates out of love in order to make of us his children. This is what is affirmed in a rarely quoted phrase of Saint Paul: God "saved us and called us with a holy calling, not according to our works but according to his own purpose and grace. This grace was given to us in Christ Jesus before all the ages began, but it has now been revealed through the appearing of our Savior Christ Jesus" (2 Tim. 1:9–10).

God's purpose and his grace were given to us in Christ Jesus before the world began. This same grace of sonship has now been revealed through the appearing of our Savior, Jesus Christ, that is, by the redemptive Incarnation of the Son for our sins, but the actual grace of filiation was prior to the Redemption. "Redemption" resides in the way sonship was given to us due to sin, but filiation is not just a response to sin, but precedes our creation itself, because it gives creation its goal (or finality) in God's design. That is why it is designated by Saint Paul as a "holy calling" (2 Tim. 1:9). This grace is the mystery of the Lamb who is blameless and spotless. It is this creative wisdom of which Saint Paul speaks: "We speak God's wisdom, secret and hidden, which God decreed before the ages for our glory. . . . But, as it is written, 'What no eye has seen, nor ear heard, nor the human heart conceived, what God has prepared for those who love him'" (1 Cor. 2:7–9). This antecedent grace, this wisdom of the mystery, contains the kingdom that will be given to us. On this subject there is a very mysterious sentence of Christ in the gospel of Saint Matthew: "Then the king will say to those at his right hand, 'Come, you that are blessed by my Father, inherit the kingdom prepared for you from the foundation of the world'" (Matt. 25:34). The kingdom is ready; it is given from the foundation of the world. It consists in this knowledge of himself that God wants all men to possess. It consists in this love, this total belonging to God, so that we can stand in his presence and be, as Saint Paul says in the hymn from the Epistle to the Ephesians, "holy and immaculate in love." Here again we have the word *immaculate*, which alludes to the spotlessness of the Lamb.

God's purpose is blameless. It is nothing but goodness. It is nothing but love. It bears no stain of compromise with evil, no reproach or limitation that would cause this love to be given only to some and not to others. It is by no means and in no way restrictive with regard to creatures. This love chooses us by drawing us out from nothingness. The sign that we are chosen is the fact that we exist; if we had not been chosen, God would not have given us being. There is no reason to go through the anxieties that tortured even some of the saints, wondering if they were elected or not. If we exist, it is because we are elected. Our existence is the sure sign of our election.

CHAPTER SIX

The Vulnerability of God as the Lamb

All is still far from having been said concerning the mystery of the Lamb. Since it is the sign of the innocence of God, since it is blameless and spotless, this Lamb also manifests in itself another aspect that is inseparable from that of innocence: namely, the extreme vulnerability of the love that God has gratuitously lavished on his kindhearted design. Almost nothing is easier than killing a lamb. It does not offer any resistance, since it is innocent. It does not imagine evil; it therefore does not anticipate the blow, which, for that very reason, is able to strike in full force. We need only recall the story of the sacrifice of Isaac and the poignant, heartrending dialogue between Abraham and Isaac as they ascend Mount Moriah. Isaac, who in this scene truly prefigures the Lamb, asks his father, "The fire and the wood are here, but where is the lamb for a burnt offering?" (Gen. 22:7). And Abraham's response is most beautiful: "God himself will provide a lamb for the burnt offering, my son" (Gen. 22:8). Everything is said but as if in a "parable" (Heb. 11:19): God will provide; that is, God will become the Lamb. Isaac is actually a figure of God himself, who, in his Son, has become the Suffering Servant: like a lamb who "did not open his mouth" and "is led to the slaughter" (Isa. 53:7).

Such is the nature of God's design that it puts the heart of the Lord who conceived it in a situation of extreme vulnerability. Because it is a design of filial adoption, it awaits a response from us. The design does not automatically presuppose that response, since, as we have seen, the initiative comes totally from God, and in that initiative, God does not consider our response in advance. But his initiative of love calls for our response and thus places itself "at our mercy."

Here our liberty will have to answer, and by its negative response it has the capacity to strike God directly in the heart, in the way that a lamb can be pierced by a blow, which it is unable to parry precisely because of its innocence.

"Let us make humankind in our image, according to our likeness" (Gen. 1:26). "*Let us*": this dialogue echoes the counsel that takes place in the Trinity. Right from the start, the liberty of man is situated at the heart of the Trinitarian counsel. The Lamb is at the heart of the Trinity, as God's kindhearted design of gratuitous love for man in his liberty. Once again this brings us back to Saint Andrew Rublev's icon of the Trinity.

God Engages His Name

Other Bible passages show that God committed his name on behalf of man. The theme of God's name is extraordinarily rich in scripture, not only in the Old Testament, but also in the New. The name is the Being of God in his most personal identity. "I am who I am" (Exod. 3:14). This designates both the Being of God and his personal freedom: *I Am*. As Israel enters progressively into a deeper intimacy with God, it discovers the divine name as a "power" that it can exert over God. When Israel invokes the Lord's name, when it asks God for something in his name, God is as if bound in relation to man. There was already an obscure prefiguration of this reality in Jacob's struggle with God at the ford of the Jabbok, when he said to the angel of the Lord, "I will not let you go, unless you bless me. . . . [T]ell me your name" (Gen. 32:26–29). But the time for that was not yet ripe. It was Moses, from the flame of the burning bush, who received the revelation of the name of his divine interlocutor: "I am who I am."

This name by which the Israelites were henceforth to invoke God, the "tetragrammaton," later became so sacred that it was considered unpronounceable. Only the high priest could utter it from behind the veil, once a year at Yom Kippur when he entered the Holiest of Holies to ask God's forgiveness. This invocation is related to another episode in the book of Exodus, when Moses intercedes for Israel after the episode of the idolatry of the golden calf. Moses goes up on the mountain, because the covenant has been broken and must be concluded again. But how can it now be reconcluded, since one of the partners, Israel, has proved itself totally unfaithful? Moses presents himself before God: "The Lord descended in the cloud and stood with him there, and proclaimed the name, 'the Lord.' The Lord passed before him, and proclaimed, *the Lord, the Lord, a God merciful and gracious, slow to anger, and abounding in steadfast love and faithfulness, keeping steadfast for the thousandth generation*" (Exod. 34:5–8).

Moses invoked the name of God, and God passed before him pronouncing his own name. In this way he restores the covenant, demonstrating the most personal source of his kindhearted design in which he has engaged himself out of love for humanity. Moses discovered the secret that consists in the invocation of the divine name. This is why the high priest, each year on Yom Kippur, after having confessed together with the people in the Temple all the faults of the nation, entered behind the veil in the Holiest of Holies. This was the only day of the year when he did so, and that was also the only day of the year when God's name was pronounced by the high priest, because this name was the unique source of forgiveness. The invocation of God's name anchors us in God's heart, in that source which, because it created us, is the only place where we can be re-created. Forgiveness signifies our reintegration into God's design. When we invoke his name, we return once again to the way in which we are seen by him in his antecedent will, and therefore evil no longer exists, since for the One Who Is, there is no evil (evil has no existence). Evil is nothing other than the destructive disorder that we cause in creation when we contradict the love of our creator.

The invocation of God's name, which in this sense is "forgiveness," fully restores to us the design of love—not in the sense of erasing the list of our sins that had been previously registered on a ledger. The name of God *is forgiveness*, just as in Saint Luke's parable the father is forgiveness when he throws himself around the prodigal child's neck without saying a word to him. It is only afterward that the prodigal son actually apologizes. The first impulse of love comes from the name of God: in the text of Exodus, it is God himself who pronounces his own name in order to forgive (Exod. 34:6).

The Last Resort

The prophets naturally came to understand this more and more through the experience of the history of Israel, especially during the tragic period that saw the prevarication of their kings, the infidelity of the people, and finally the siege of Jerusalem and the deportation to Babylon. As the nation sank deeper and deeper into the night, the prophets realized that they could not invoke anything before God. Whom could they put forth as a claim for mercy? David, the foundation of the monarchy, represented by kings who had behaved monstrously? Abraham, father of an unfaithful nation? Moses, whose Law had been trampled? How was it possible to invoke any of these names before God? Who then was to be invoked before God? But the prophets then come upon the secret wellspring that Moses had discovered on Sinai, and they began to invoke God himself by his name. This brings us back again to that great intuition that often brought Saint Thomas Aquinas to tears when singing the liturgical responsory *Media vita*: "In the middle of our lives, we are already at the threshold of death, and to whom shall we go for help, if not to yourself, O Lord, you, who have been justly provoked to wrath by our sins: Holy God, Holy Mighty One, Holy and Merciful Savior." It is to you, before whom we are nothing but sin, it is to you alone that we can turn in search of salvation. Although his very presence highlights our sins, it is still to him alone that we can turn looking for forgiveness. But he gives us more than forgiveness, he actually re-creates us, because in him we become such as he wants us to be in the love and the glory of his name: "Although our iniquities testify against us, act, O Lord, for your name's sake" (Jer. 14:7). "We are called by your name; do not forsake us" (Jer. 14:9). "Do not spurn us, for your name's sake. . . .

[R]emember and do not break your covenant with us" (Jer. 14:21). In the prophet Baruch, we find the same memorial of the name in the great penitential prayer of those who were in exile: "Do not remember the iniquities of our ancestors, but in this crisis remember your power and your name" (Bar. 3:5).

Ezekiel, who is writing in the context of the exile, after the people had been deprived of their rights, their land, and their temple, turns toward God. The Lord speaks to him, and after recalling the long history of Israel's infidelities, he declares, "Then I thought I would pour out my wrath on them and spend my anger against them in the midst of the land of Egypt. But I acted for the sake of my name, that it should not be profaned in the sight of the nations among whom they lived, in whose sight I made myself known to them in bringing them out of the land of Egypt" (Ezek. 20:8–9). Ezekiel 36:21 reiterates: "I had concern for my holy name. . . ." In Ezekiel the Lord also says, "I scattered them among the nations, and they were dispersed through the countries; in accordance with their conduct and their deeds I judged them. But when they came to the nations, wherever they came, they profaned my holy name, in that it was said of them, 'These are the people of the Lord, and yet they had to go out of his land'" (Ezek. 36:19–20).

That which affects Israel, that which affects humanity as God wants it to be, also affects the glory of the name of God, who has committed himself in virtue of a promise. In the covenant, God has committed something very deep within himself, the fidelity of his love, the love that has its source in his very being.

> I had concern for my holy name, which the house of Israel had profaned among the nations to which they came. Therefore say to the house of Israel, Thus says the Lord God: It is not for your sake, O house of Israel, that I am about to act, but for the sake of my holy name, which you have profaned among the nations to which you came. I will sanctify my great name, which has been profaned among the nations, and which you have profaned among them; and the nations shall know that I am the Lord, says the Lord God, when through you I display my holiness before their eyes. I will take you from the nations, and gather you from all the countries, and bring you into your

own land. I will sprinkle clean water upon you, and you shall be clean from all your uncleannesses, and from all your idols I will cleanse you. A new heart I will give you, and a new spirit I will put within you; and I will remove from your body the heart of stone and give you a heart of flesh. (Ezek. 36:21–26)

In Ezekiel, this very central passage concerning the promise is attached to the name of God. In deference to his name, God will restore his covenant in a manner that already directly announces the mystery of Emmanuel. The same perception is expressed in one of the Psalms: "Help us, O God of our salvation, for the glory of your name; deliver us, and forgive our sins, for your name's sake" (Ps. 79:9). We are sinners, but if God were not to remain true to himself, even in the face of our sins, it is his own name that would suffer detriment. Paul himself says, "If we are faithless, he remains faithful—for he cannot deny himself" (2 Tim. 2:13). He cannot deny himself: this is the name that is engaged in the mystery of the Lamb. God is bound by his own innocence. This innocence causes his love to be both infinitely vulnerable in relation to our response and terribly obstinate, because he himself has engaged his own name.

In the last part of the book of Isaiah, after the exile, this name begins to emerge as the name of the Father. "Look down from heaven and see, from your holy and glorious habitation. Where are your zeal and your might? The yearning of your heart and your compassion? They are withheld from me. For you are our father, though Abraham does not know us and Israel does not acknowledge us; you, O Lord, are our father; our Redeemer from of old is your name" (Isa. 63:15–16). Father, such is your name. These words lead us to the threshold of the "Our Father" such as it was given to us by Christ when he revealed to us a fatherhood that is much more radical than that of Abraham and Israel. Even if they deny us because we have been completely unfaithful to the covenant they concluded with you, you are our father in a much more essential way, and in your paternity there is the mystery of love that is faithful against all odds. Such is the mystery of the Lamb, the mystery of a God who is innocent and vulnerable; and his vulnerability, because it belongs to his innocence, is extremely obstinate: God cannot forget man with whom he has fallen in love once and for all.

Man in the Heart of God

Man has always been present in the design of God. In the Old Testament the angel of the Lord who appears in Genesis to Abraham at the Oak of Mamre, to Jacob at the ford of the Jabbok, and to Moses in the burning bush has a human shape. This is very surprising in the Jewish context, where idolatry is formally condemned and where human representations of God are strictly prohibited by the Law. Nevertheless, these ancient texts show a human manifestation of God in the mystery of the angel of the Lord, who is God himself. He has a human form, as if God carried in himself the prototype of the man whom he created in his image; as if he carried in himself in his design, this image of man, such as he wants him to be. And when he appeared to man, he already manifested himself to him in this image.

The church fathers considered these Old Testament apparitions of God in human form to be anticipated manifestations of the mystery of Christ. That, for example, is the way in which they understood Christ's words about Abraham: "He saw [my day] and was glad" (John 8:56). Abraham saw Christ's day when, at the Oak of Mamre, the angel of the Lord came to announce the birth of Isaac, and Sara laughed and rejoiced. The angel of the Lord who comes, who is God himself, already has the human face of the Son, whose Incarnation was prepared by the promise of an offspring in the person of Isaac.

The prophets of the last period, starting from Ezekiel and going through the exile, all had the presentiment of this. The book of Ezekiel opens with an astonishing vision. Ezekiel sees the glory of God, God himself on his throne placed on a chariot of fire. He describes the living creatures, the angels who carry as if on wheels of fire a crystal throne; and on this throne someone is seated. This someone, who is going to be described, is, of course, God himself: "Above the dome that was over their heads [of the symbolic animals, representing the angelic world] there was something like a throne, in appearance like sapphire; and seated above the likeness of a throne [designating the position of God] was something that seemed like a human form" (Ezek. 1:26). This is something unheard of and staggering in the context of the Old Testament, where any icon or pictorial representation is still unthinkable because it would have been qualified as idolatry. But here the prophet sees the manifestation of the glory of God in human form, that is, through his design of love for man.

Similarly Zechariah sees "the angel of the Lord standing among the myrtle trees" (Zech. 1:11) who gives orders to the other angels sent to patrol the earth (Zech. 1:10), as "a man riding on a red horse . . . among the myrtle trees in the glen" (Zech. 1:8). Now this "angel of the Lord" has a human figure, unlike the other angels whom he governs. He also has a personal relationship with the "Lord of hosts" with whom he intercedes for men (Zech. 1:12). Later on, Zechariah suggests a link between this mysterious humanity of the angel of the Lord, in whom he does not fail to sense the presence of God himself, and the Messianic fulfillment of the prophecies in the offspring of David: "On that day . . . the house of David shall be like God, like the angel of the Lord, at their head" (Zech. 12:8).

The prophet Daniel takes one more step in the same direction as Zechariah. In Daniel, the heavenly figure of the Son of Man is already beginning to distinguish itself, within the divine sphere of heaven, from the One who is the Ancient of Days, the Father. We are already in the most immediate foreshadowing of the mystery of the Son who is clothed with the design concerning man: "I watched in the night visions, I saw one like a human being coming with the clouds of heaven. And he came to the Ancient One and was presented before him. To him was given dominion and glory and kingship, that all peoples, nations, and languages should serve him. His dominion is an everlasting dominion that shall not pass away, and his kingship is one that shall never be destroyed" (Dan. 7:13–14).

The "Insides" of God's Tender Mercy

The human form that the Son of Man carries in the very heart of God indicates the degree to which man is related to the name of God. God has committed his most personal mystery, his name, to his design of love for man. This gives us an idea of just how vulnerable God's love is in that design. This vulnerability is already expressed in a very beautiful way in two particularly moving Old Testament passages. The first is from Isaiah: "Zion said, 'The Lord has forsaken me, my Lord has forgotten me.' Can a woman forget her nursing child, or show no compassion for the child of her womb? Even these may forget, yet I will not forget you. See, I have inscribed you on the palms of my hands" (Isa. 49:14–16). *I have inscribed you on the palms of my hands*: this scriptural image was employed by the church fathers to evoke the stigmata of Christ, the nail holes in his flesh. *I have inscribed you on the palms of my hands*; this was true right down to its extreme realization on the cross. This Semitic expression means that what a person wears engraved on the palm of his hands touches him personally. In the Song of Solomon, the bride says, "Set me as a seal upon your arm" (8:6). The beloved is inscribed in that which is infinitely vulnerable, the palm of the hand. Here too the mystery of the Lamb is already revealed.

The other passage is in Zechariah, the prophet of the "one who is pierced": "Thus says the Lord of hosts (after his glory sent me), regarding the nations that plundered you: Truly, one who touches you touches the apple of my eye" (Zech 2:8). The apple of the eye. Is it possible to imagine anything more sensitive or more vulnerable than that? This is what man is for God in his design of love. Hosea had already situated Ephraim in the "insides" of God. He uses this expression to indicate the profound level of vulnerability at which God carries man. "My people are bent on turning away from me. To the Most High they call, but he does not raise them up at all. How can I give you up, O Ephraim? How can I hand you over, O Israel? How can I make you like Admah? How can I treat you like Zeboiim? My heart recoils within me; my compassion grows warm and tender. I will not execute my fierce anger; I will not again destroy Ephraim; for I am God and no mortal, the Holy One in your midst, and I will not come in wrath" (Hosea 11:7–9). This is a truly astounding passage. God, precisely because of his name, on behalf of his holiness, feels his *insides* quiver and cannot destroy Ephraim as the latter's infidelity would deserve. "If we are faithless, he remains faithful—for he cannot deny himself," says Saint Paul (2 Tim. 2:13).

But the mystery of the kindhearted design of God's love, which is as faithful as it is vulnerable, is not expressed in the figure of a *slain* lamb. The text of Saint Peter does not say that the Lamb is slain or offered in sacrifice. Saint Peter says here that the Lamb "destined before the foundation of the world" is "without defect or blemish," but before the foundation of the world it was not yet *slain or sacrificed*. Before the foundation of the world, in the antecedent will of God's plan, it does not appear as slain or sacrificed; it is known as an innocent and vulnerable Lamb, the figure of the faithful love in which God commits his name. Therefore we cannot yet speak of a wound, since this wound did not necessarily have to occur. God conceived his design in such a way, and he committed himself to it in such a way, that he exposed himself as the Lamb: his innocence became infinitely vulnerable. Why? Because this design comes entirely from the heart of God; this design of kindhearted love can only be accomplished with our consent, as adoptive sonship must respect our liberty. God's purpose is not to make slaves happy by giving them plenty to eat or by treating them well. His purpose is to lead sons to the discovery of the heart of the Father.

The Possibility Liberty Has of Hardening Itself

This brings us back to the drama, mentioned earlier, of the prodigal son. In this parable we see sin represented by two things: the prodigal son asks his father for "his portion of the inheritance," and he requests this in order to be able to leave and enjoy it by himself, away from the father. It did not even come into his mind that his father wanted to share the entire inheritance with him now. He asks for his portion of the inheritance. Our sin splits up the inheritance of God, so that we can snatch something away from the Lord and enjoy it, not together with him, but alone by ourselves. In this way we inevitably deprive ourselves of the entire inheritance, and we finally end up by squandering even the portion that we carry away, because we condemn it to death by detaching it from its creative source.

But the elder and apparently more "faithful" son also fails to recognize the father's heart. That is why, returning from the fields, he is scandalized by the banquet given to welcome back his younger brother. Here is the reproach that he addresses to his father: "I have served you every day, but you have never given me a young goat to celebrate with my friends." He, in his slavish loyalty, did not understand the love of the father. He was hoping for a goat in order to celebrate with his friends but not with the father. He had the same attitude as the prodigal son, but he was more timid and therefore did not dare go as far as his brother. And so he served but as a slave; he did not love in a way that befits a son.

The great drama is that our liberty can frustrate God's design for us. "If we deny him, he will also deny us" (2 Tim. 2:12), not out of vengeance or spite, but because he is obliged to respect the last word of our freedom. Respecting our liberty, "remaining faithful because he cannot deny himself," implies that he cannot stop loving us and that he would be obliged to pursue us forever with his love even if a definitive "no" on our part were to interpose itself between his love and us. How else is it possible to represent damnation, other than as God's love eternally pursuing the damned who are opposed to this love, because they have rendered themselves forever resistant to it and have taken it into such disgust that it has literally become their "hell"?

It is impossible to conceive that God could cease to love one of his creatures. Hell is not a place on the outside where God would relegate the damned, far away from his love; hell can only reside inside the liberty of the one who damns himself. The person who is damned, as Saint Simeon the New Theologian sensed in the hymns he wrote about himself and his own sin, is surrounded by light, but he changes that light into his own inner darkness. This is not because he is no longer inundated with light or because God has withdrawn his love; no, it is because he himself transforms this light into darkness. God cannot be unfaithful, even in the face of this final denial. But he cannot remove this denial; he cannot suppress the liberty which is inseparable from the dignity of a child of God. Here we come up against the "mystery of lawlessness" (2 Thess. 2:7) as a possible frustration of God's purpose. This possible contradiction of God's design is manifested in the Lamb by its extreme vulnerability. This extreme vulnerability, however, is inseparable from the strength of its faithfulness because its bones cannot be broken.

Several passages of scripture illustrate the redoubtable power that man has, in his liberty, to contradict God's love and to thus render vain his kindhearted design: "But by refusing to be baptized by [John the Baptist]," Jesus declared, "the Pharisees and lawyers rejected God's purpose for themselves" (Luke 7:30). This is not to say that the design does not exist or that God had excluded them from it in advance; nor does it mean that God withdrew his purpose starting from the moment when they rejected it. It means instead that they have defeated the design of God in them and prevented it from bearing any fruit: this is a redoubtable possibility that should fill us with fear concerning our own liberty and the immense respect that God owes to himself in his design, which requires that he respect our liberty. He is obliged to pursue our liberty with his love, but he always pursues it precisely as liberty. He would not have access to it if he were to change it into something other than that which it is, a person's liberty. He can only pursue that liberty from within, not by any external manipulation.

The Book of Life in the Hands of the Lamb

Such is the mystery of the book of life, mentioned in the book of Revelation: "If you conquer, you will be clothed like them in white robes, and I will not blot your name out of the book of life; I will confess your name before my Father and before his angels" (Rev. 3:5). The book of life is not a book in which our names are written in advance, a book in which only some names are written and others are not; it is the book of the eternal knowledge of God that coincides with the present of our liberty. Although we have been destined by God to take part in his divine life, we can "erase our names from the book of life" by rendering his love vain. This is why, in Revelation, the book of life appears in the hands of the Lamb. The Lamb carries our liberty in the loving design of God, "inscribed on the palms of his hands," "posed as a seal upon his heart," "immersed deeply in the *insides* of in his tender mercy," according to the various images that evoke this reality in scripture.

The Lamb, who has been *discerned* by God before the foundation of the world, possesses all the elements that make possible the sacrifice of Christ, but this sacrifice was in no way a predetermined necessity. The Lamb's extreme vulnerability did not inevitably have to be wounded. The Lamb was discerned by God, but it was not yet slain. The Lamb is slain not *before the foundation of the world* but *from the beginning of the world*, from the moment when man, through the original sin, inflicts the first and most radical wound on the loving design of God for him; this is the wound that all our sins will ratify from generation to generation. It is because of this that we are led to the sacrificial modality through which God is henceforth going to accomplish the mystery of the Lamb. But even if we had not sinned, the eternal Son would have been given to us as a Lamb in his wedding with humanity. The Lamb would always have been an absolutely essential dimension of God's love for us, because God's design took the form of an adoption of our liberty, which is engraved in God's heart. Even if the response of our love had been entirely positive from the start, the folly of God's love for us would still have taken the form of the Lamb. But it is not necessary to introduce sacrifice as an absolutely essential element in the mystery of the Lamb. This mystery consists substantially in the "folly" of a God who falls in love with his creature and who wants to lead this creature to deification from the depths of its own liberty.

Even for a humanity that would have been without sin like the Virgin Mary, God would have been a Lamb but not a slain Lamb. He would have been a Lamb because of the innocence and vulnerability of his design for us.

PART TWO

The Economy of the Mystery

The accomplishment of the kindhearted design through the contradictions of evil

O Lord, my Mercy, what is to become of sinners?
—Saint Dominic

There is not, never has been, and never will be a single human being for whom Christ did not suffer.
—Council of Quiercy (853)

CHAPTER SEVEN

The Son as the Lamb Who Was Slain from the Beginning of the World

Let me summarize what I have said so far: in the Trinity, the Son is the Lamb eternally, in the strongest sense of the term. The Lamb is of course God: the three divine persons are the Lamb because the three are Love, and therefore each participates in the same kindhearted design. But one of the three is "clothed" in the Lamb as the only begotten Son, who carries and guarantees the design of adoptive sonship. This design has to be accomplished in him. He is the one who says the "Amen"; he is ultimately the blameless and spotless Lamb, "destined before the foundation of the world." It is in and through the Son that a humanity that had not sinned would have discovered the vulnerable heart of the Father in which the Son dwells. Mankind would have had to grow (just as the Virgin Mary did, she who was without sin) in the knowledge of God's merciful and infinitely vulnerable heart; it would have been a little like what we see when spouses who love each other grow together without betraying their love: the more they advance, the more they realize what a vulnerable thing their love is. The more one enters into love, the more one realizes how fragile it is and how the least little thing would be enough to hurt it or damage it. Although we do not know how it would have come about in a sinless world, it still would have been the mystery of the Lamb, the mystery of God's innocence, the mystery of the Lord falling in love with our liberty in the "folly" of his goodness. He would have caused our liberty to grow progressively in an ever more delicate response until the final "Amen," said in perfect conformity with the only begotten Son, which would have established us forever in God's eternity.

Alas, we discovered love in the worst possible way: we came to know it only by wounding it. It is a great mistake to believe that we need to hurt another person in order to have proof that we are loved by him: liberty is in fact capable of inventing so many other better and more wonderful ways of discovering how much we are loved.

And therefore, because of our sin, the Lamb was slain. Not "before the foundation of the world," since, according to Saint Peter's expression, the Lamb is only said to have been foreknown as "without defect or blemish" before the world's foundation; but the Lamb is slain "from the foundation of the world," since it is starting from the original sin at the origin of humanity that the covenant between God and man was broken. This is affirmed in the book of Revelation in a passage concerning the "worshipers of the beast" at the end of time: "All the inhabitants of the earth will worship it [the beast], everyone whose name has not been written in the book of life of the Lamb that was slaughtered from the foundation of the world" (Rev. 13:8).[1] This is the literal translation of the Greek text, but it seems that most translators hesitated when confronted with the unusual idea that "the Lamb was slaughtered from the foundation of the world," and they therefore often attempted to change the order of the words in the Greek, translating instead: "All the inhabitants of the earth will worship it [the beast], everyone whose name has not been written from the foundation of the world in the book of life of the Lamb that was slaughtered."[2] But the Greek text really does say "the Lamb was slaughtered from the foundation of the world": "from the foundation of the world" relates grammatically to "the Lamb [who] was slaughtered," not directly to the names that are written or not written in the book of life.

As I said earlier, the book of life is not some sort of register where God, in his love, would enroll in advance certain names, those of the "elect," while rejecting and abandoning others, those of the reprobate. In another passage from the same book of Revelation, Christ pronounces a warning that formally contradicts the idea of any divine condemnation prior to sin on man's part: "If you conquer . . . I will not blot your name out of the book of life; I will confess your name before my Father and before his angels" (Rev. 3:5). It is therefore we who can erase ourselves because of our sins from the book of life, where our names have been inscribed by God "who desires everyone to be saved" (1 Tim. 2:4).

The Lamb is slain from the foundation of the world because of these same erasures in the book of life, erasures due to sin that began "at the origins of the world"; for God is bound by his design, he cannot deny himself: he promised us the Son, so the Son must be given to us. But now the Son must wed our humanity in an entirely different way by actually taking it upon himself. Through his Incarnation, he comes to us as the Redeemer who substitutes himself in our place. He does not come now simply to recapitulate our "Amen" by adding to it his own ultimate revelation; he must now also say that "Amen" in our place. All this requires that he be "born of a woman" (Gal. 4:4), that is, in an individual way, with a particular human nature, apparently as just one more individual of the human species; it also requires that he be "born under the law," that is, in a human nature stigmatized by the mortality and frailties that are the consequences of sin.

But this is not the scenario that God wanted in his initial or primary will, in the very first movement of his heart. It is we, through our sin, who have caused the scenario of redemption: as the creed says, "for our salvation he came down from heaven." God proceeds in order to implement his unchanging purpose, which is to introduce us into his paternity through the Son in the Spirit. But now it must enter a human mass that has become darkness because of its resistance to the "Amen." In his design, God comes up against the contradiction of evil.

Starting from the rupture of the origins, the Lamb is slain. That which, in the Lord's kindhearted design, was merely vulnerability has now become a wound, for now sin has actually inflicted that wound. Sin, which was neither necessary nor anticipated, is the dark side of the Tree of Life; it is the Tree of the Knowledge of Good and Evil. It is the imagination of evil, that is, the conception of a false growth in the Good, a disorder with regard to the Good, the illusion of self-fulfillment in happiness apart from God. The parable of the prodigal son shows us a humanity that wants its own portion of the inheritance, in order to enjoy it away from the Father, far from his heart. Man is thus left with an inheritance that has been fragmented, and for that very reason it has also been squandered and dilapidated.

The Flouting of the Lord's Gratuitous Love

It is now that the secret of the Lamb appears, the mystery of his strength and his weakness: God takes hold of the unacceptable. Evil is for God the one absolutely unacceptable thing, because it is a pure lie, a lie that produces a truly destructive nightmare. God who is Being, who is Love, who is Goodness, cannot resign himself to evil. In him there is not the least shadow of any resignation to evil: his "victorious acceptance" of that which is unacceptable is the very opposite of resignation. God does not for a moment accept evil by surrendering to it. Through his innocence, God, who does not conceive evil, goes ahead stubbornly in the Good, taking the unique way that he knows, even to the point of colliding head-on with evil: he will continue to pursue man with his love. But in order to redeem man, who, in his liberty, turned away from the Lord by deliberately introducing into his own heart the fissure of evil, God comes up against that which is unacceptable. The wound of divine Love that results from this has nothing to do with our human injuries. The love of God that has been flouted is a totally gratuitous love. The fact of being flouted in a purely gratuitous love does not diminish God in any way, because God *is* Being. God does not possess being as something that could be taken away from him; he simply is. He is totally poor in his being because it is not for him something that he "possesses." But for that very reason, he cannot lose anything. The fullness of Being is infinitely poor in its simplicity: nothing can be taken away from it, because it *has* nothing; but at the same time, it *is* everything. Although we can try to withdraw water from a fountain, we can in no way diminish the intensity of the flowing jet because it is the outpouring of a total gift: even though we draw some of the water, the source is in no way affected by this; it continues to flow and is not deprived of anything. A source, like the pure love offered as an entirely free gift, bears no scars from the "injuries" that are inflicted on it.

This image is of course only an approximation, because in fact, at one point some of the water is removed from the source. Nevertheless, it gives a fairly good representation of God as the source of the Being, of God whose love cannot know any suffering, since suffering always implies a deprivation. In us, because we are creatures, being does not come first. Our being is only something that we possess, as a gift in which we have a share, but we *are not* the Being. God alone *is* the Being (Being in its fullness), and that is why he alone can give being to others as the creator. It is impossible therefore for him to be wounded in himself, although he can be wounded in that which is like "the apple of his eye," that is, in us whom he wants for ourselves and to whom he has given himself as our ultimate end.

An example will perhaps give us insight into what a wound can be for divine love. Imagine parents whose adolescent child has turned bad and who one day steals from them. Will the father and mother suffer over the loss of some of their goods and the injustice done to them due to this, or will they suffer because their child has become a thief? They will obviously suffer principally because of what their child has become, at least if they are true parents worthy of the name. They could address their child quoting the words of the father in the prodigal son parable: "All that is mine is yours." And they could add, "Why did you not ask us instead of just taking things for yourself?" It is through self-degradation that a child can most grievously wound his parents. The more a love is gratuitous, the more it resides in the loved one rather than in the person who loves. And when this is the case, the person who loves tends to feel less suffering himself while being able to more efficaciously help the loved one.

Here is the ultimate feature of God's omnipotent paternity: not only does the Father not anticipate the unforeseeable choices of our liberty, not only does he accept the unacceptable represented by our sins, not only does he allow himself to be wounded in the heart of his gratuitous love when we refuse that love, but going further, he victoriously seizes that wound, not allowing it to affect his love for us. He takes hold of it entirely and envelops it in a greater love, a superabundance of grace, as Saint Paul says: "where sin increased, grace abounded all the more" (Rom. 5:20).

The only scar caused by the wounds we inflict on God's design is a superabundance of love. God, theologians tell us, cannot suffer any deprivation because as the Almighty Father, he is the source of Being, that is, of Being that is eternally given in love. For this reason, he can in no way lack anything. Although for us, affectivity is inseparable from the idea of love, emotional passion implies, in reality, not a greater love, but something that affects us and therefore diminishes and takes away the strength we need to love effectively. The emotional dimension that in us, as creatures, cannot be separated from love actually diminishes some of the effectiveness of that love. It prevents us from giving ourselves totally in love. The more our love allows itself to be affected by failure or by suffering, the less strength it has to be effective, to work actively and in truth.

Impassibility of God in a Pure and Total Gift

Once again let us try to grasp this through an image, or rather through a true story that helped me personally perceive the truth of this victorious love of God that does not allow itself to be discouraged or even affected, precisely because it is a totally generous and gratuitous love. I once found myself in the presence of a mother at the bedside of her child. The latter, suffering from a serious type of poisoning, struggled for forty-eight hours between life and death. In this battle marked by tetanic convulsions, the child suffered tremendously. The mother was at his bedside to support him physically and morally. Now someone who was simply passing by said to her, "How painful it must be for you to see your child suffer in this way!" But she made this surprising answer: "Me suffer? I don't have time for that." These surprising words are actually quite understandable. For a mother in those circumstances suffering would have involved turning in upon herself and focusing on her own feelings rather than on devoting herself entirely to her child; it would have meant depriving the child of a part of her love. It would have deprived him of a love that is entirely benevolent or beneficial in act and in truth. Her suffering was in fact entirely spent in the care that she gave to her child. It passed into her hand as she took the hand of the child, into her eyes that she laid upon him, into her smile and into her solicitude for all his needs. In all this, she was not remaining in herself; she was not suffering in herself; she was not "affected" by the suffering. Her love, with all its energy and strength, had become entirely active.

No, it is hardly possible for us to suffer in ourselves when we give of ourselves to such an extreme degree. We are totally seized by the suffering of the other person. Our love that responds totally to the loved one's call of distress becomes like a source unable to lose anything, because whatever is taken away only increases the intensity and speed with which it flows. Who can discern the hollow spot made by a bucket that draws water from a freely flowing source? "Where sin increased, grace abounded all the more."

God's love bears no scars. In him there can be no wound due to a lack of owning something, because he is Being, and it is impossible to remove anything from a love that has given everything. Where then are the wounds of divine love? Precisely in the creatures whom he has adopted as his children. We injure the gratuitousness of God's love by refusing his gifts and by depriving ourselves of them. In this sense it is we who are open wounds in the benevolent design of divine love for us.

This is what God wanted to show us in the Incarnation. A human nature like unto our own, in its hypostatic union with the only begotten Son, was needed in order to manifest the Lamb who takes upon himself the sins of the world: "He himself bore our sins in his body on the cross," says Saint Peter (1 Pet. 2:24), in a passage that refers freely to Isaiah's song of the Suffering Servant (Isa. 53:4–9, 11–12). Saint Matthew also refers to this same passage of Isaiah when commenting on the Lord's first collective miraculous cures toward the beginning of his gospel: "They brought to him [Jesus] many who were possessed . . . and he cast out the spirits with a word, and cured all who were sick. This was to fulfill what had been spoken through the prophet Isaiah, 'He took our infirmities and bore our diseases'" (Matt. 8:16–17, referring to Isa. 53:4).

By taking on, in the person of his Son, a human nature like our own, and which is therefore capable of being expressed in terms of lacking and suffering, the wound inflicted on his gratuitous love, God wanted us to see, translated into flesh and blood, all that sin represents for his love: the blow that struck the Lamb but that could not break his bones, because these bones are the divine mystery of being and love from which nothing can be taken away; and yet that Lamb may be wounded in his heart. Simultaneously and inseparably, he is all force and all vulnerability.

The Revelation of the Transfixed Heart

Christ's human suffering is only the created translation of the offense experienced by divine love that has been flouted. We are tempted to think that God needed the humanity of Christ to discover a more merciful love through suffering. In fact the exact opposite is true, and this is clearly manifested when Jesus's side is pierced with a spear. Saint Catherine addresses the Lord in this way: "My sweetly beloved Lamb, you were already dead when your side was opened. Why then did you want your heart to be wounded and opened so that it would shed blood so abundantly?" And Jesus answers her: "I wanted this opening in my side to reveal to you the secret of my heart, because my heart contained more love for man than that which the body could manifest while it was alive."

Not only did the human nature assumed by the Son not increase his divine love, but his limited humanity could really only be an imperfect expression of his unlimited love. Jesus said to Saint Catherine of Siena, "My desire for men was infinite, and the present act of suffering and torment was finite. Therefore through this suffering I could not entirely show you how much I loved you, because my love was infinite. That is why I wanted to reveal to you the secret of my heart, by allowing you to see it opened, so that you could understand that it loved you more than it was able to prove by its finite suffering." Even after his human death, his heart had to be pierced so that the mystery of the Lamb could appear: God pierced or transfixed in his love by sin, since the beginning of the world.

Thus Christ's suffering cannot be measured in neurological terms. It may be that in the course of history some people have been subjected to more terrible tortures than those inflicted on Christ. That is not unthinkable. But the question is not there, because the mystery of Christ's suffering stems entirely from Gethsemane where his true agony took place. This suffering comes entirely from inside of Christ, from the divine, and it is expressed outwardly in a human fashion. The first blood that Christ shed, the blood of his agony, was not shed due to any physical blow; it flowed from Christ's body like perspiration, coming from the very depths of the union of his humanity with his divine person. This blood of the agony expresses in terms of human suffering the contradiction stemming from that which is unacceptable for the divine love that has been flouted.

Saint Catherine of Siena continues, saying, "Love is infinite, but the punishment he underwent was finite; therefore, the cross of desire was more cruel than that of the body." No human suffering, not even that of Christ, can give the full measure of this, because that measure is divine; it is the true measure of the love in which we are loved. And therefore it was necessary that the actual heart of the God-man be pierced or transfixed, as the focal point of his personal identity, which signifies the hypostatic union of the only begotten Son with humanity and, in this humanity, with all of us whose sins he was carrying.

Divine love, a love that is totally innocent, a love that is vulnerable but also faithful even unto to the point of obstinacy, has victoriously taken hold of the contradiction of sin by which it has been flouted. It goes out to meet this contradiction; the Lamb goes forward to encounter the blow. God in his love has taken hold of sin, which is the complete contradiction of his love. How came it to be that the innocent and Holy One, who is totally alien to sin, to the point of not having any idea of evil and of not being able to conceive evil in advance even as a possibility, has now become the Lamb who carries the sin of the world?

CHAPTER EIGHT

Gethsemane

The Supreme Contradiction of Evil

Our eyes will now focus on the vessel that contains the Lamb in Rublev's icon: *the cup*. This cup reveals the mystery of the agony at Gethsemane where divine Love, which had been rejected and flouted, resonated so strongly in the humanity of the Son through whom it was expressed. We should note that it is at Gethsemane that the gospel speaks of an "agony" and not when Christ is dying on the cross. *Agony* in Greek means "struggle," and the Gethsemane episode is indeed about struggle: the struggle of divine love that goes out to encounter the radical contradiction of sin in order to completely take hold of it, to the point that Paul can say that Christ became "sin" and "malediction" for us. Christ wants to take hold of the contradiction of sin by the force of his innocence, in his obstinate fidelity, without ever conceiving it as evil. For this reason he is stricken, wounded, and contradicted by it all the more.

We have here the direct opposite of "dolorism," an attitude that would invite us to live the divine event of Gethsemane or of the cross by intensely focusing on the human element, the suffering, the quantifiable aspect of Christ's pain. Doing this gives rise to a spirituality that seeks to "comfort" the Lord in his human experience of deprivation. Here, on the contrary, we enter into the night of Gethsemane as into the cell of divine mercy, which is the place of *our consolation*. This may seem scandalous. Nevertheless, it constitutes the ultimate revelation of the love with which we have been loved. Saint Catherine of Siena drew from it the hope of the salvation of souls against all human hope, when she came face-to-face with the contradiction of evil constituted by sin. She knew that in God's heart, which was revealed through the agony of Gethsemane, the liberty of man was accepted by the Lord but not with resignation. God took hold of it in a victorious manner; he took hold of this "no" to make it a "yes" of our liberties. Therefore this human and divine drama, far from being reduced to the physical pain endured by Christ, takes on universal dimensions. The Lamb is slain from the foundation of the world, that is, starting from the original sin, and Christ, as Pascal said, remains in agony until the end of the world. The Lamb is slain for as long as there remains a single human liberty that says "no"; and thus he is sacrificed forever in the mystery of the damnation of the devil, and in those men who eventually may choose to follow the demon to the end, in refusing to be loved by God.

The mystery of the Lamb expresses the nonresignation of God to evil, the obstinacy of God, the hand-to-hand combat between God and the evil that he cannot conceive. "The light shines in the darkness, and darkness did not overcome it" (John 1:5). This struggle highlights Being and its contradiction, two opponents who cannot recognize each other in their innermost motivations. For evil, properly speaking, does not exist, it *is not*: it is identifiable only as a cancerous parasite of the good, the disorder introduced into the good by the revolt of a created person's liberty. We can, by choosing evil, cause the growth of that which is good to become cancerous and disorderly, turning it into something monstrous; instead of inducing the being received from the creator to truly grow and flourish, we can squander and destroy it.

When God takes hold of the unacceptable contradiction that sin represents for him, he in fact takes hold of our liberty. He struggles with evil, but he knows perfectly well that evil does not exist, and therefore, in fact, he is struggling with us. Because we really do exist and our liberty, which was meant to be the place of the conjugal union of humanity with God, has become the battlefield where we exploit that which we have received from God in order to resist his love. The only weapons we have to use against God are the very gifts he has given us, because by ourselves we have nothing: evil can only "create" nothingness.

The Fra Angelico icon shows us that the mystery of the Lamb who is slain is the mystery of the holiness of God who is enthroned in majesty, blindfolded, carrying the world in his hand, while also taking hold of the contradiction of his love by the evil that he cannot conceive but that he nevertheless takes up in order to draw from it a good. The Lord cannot conceive evil as evil, because evil is a "no" and God is nothing but "yes." He cannot conceive of it, just as light cannot have an idea of the darkness that it illuminates, and just as dark shadows cannot overcome the light on which they fall.

The Supreme Temptation of God

We must not forget that the agony of Jesus at Gethsemane is presented in the gospel as the supreme temptation. Here is how Saint Luke concludes of the episode of Christ's temptations in the desert: "When the devil had finished every test, he departed from him until an opportune time" (Luke 4:13). We need to clearly understand what the temptations in the desert are before we can correctly interpret the temptation of Gethsemane. We must never forget that the person of Jesus, the subject who designates himself as "I" or "me," is the Son of God who has come in the flesh. In Jesus, there is no human subject superimposed on the person of the Son who is the second person of the Trinity: when Jesus says "I," it is the Son of God who speaks; this of course happens through a human psychology that serves as an instrument for him to manifest himself to men. It is important to keep this in mind to understand the temptations of Jesus in the desert, and even more the temptation of Gethsemane, all of which are radically different from what we call "temptation."

Temptation for us occurs when evil is suggested to our imagination, placing our liberty between the true good and a good that is illusory because it is disordered. We are all familiar with the resulting oscillation. It is the psychological experience of hesitation, or of vacillating back and forth, that we call "temptation." Nothing, absolutely nothing, in the gospel allows us to detect any such oscillation in Jesus's liberty. When the Lord is tempted in the desert, he responds calmly to the devil by quoting scripture. His temptations resemble ours only in their subject matter; having perceived that Jesus is hungry, that he is without human power and that he even seems to be without any manifest divine power, the devil tempts the Lord with regard to these diverse forms of human weakness. The demon focuses on the "condition of the slave" that the Son of God has taken upon himself. The devil tempts him in order to submit him to a "test," in an effort to discover more about the person with whom he is dealing. The demon has absolutely no knowledge of the mystery of the Incarnation; he completely excluded himself from this knowledge by his rejection of God's love in God's kindhearted design for man. Nevertheless, Satan senses that God's power is present in Jesus. By his temptations, starting from the most basic or common form of human weakness constituted by hunger and ending with the apparent weakness of this "Servant of God" who does not show his power by any spectacular act, the devil tries to find out who Jesus is. In a certain sense he picks up an important clue after the third temptation when Jesus declares, "It is said, 'Do not put the Lord your God to the test'" (Luke 4:12). This last reply of Jesus, drawn from Deuteronomy, shows that, in fact, through that which is human, Satan always tries to tempt God himself. And now he actually finds himself in the presence of God. And thus he exhausted or used up every temptation, as the text of Luke says: "When the devil had finished every test, he departed from him until an opportune time" (Luke 4:13).

How are we to understand this passage that seems almost contradictory? Every temptation was exhausted, every temptation playing on that which is human and relating to the weakness of human nature. Satan now realizes that Jesus is not a man like all the others whom he could attack in their weak point, in their liberty that was capable of separating itself from God. Henceforth in his confrontation with Christ, Satan will have to fall back on a register of temptation that aims at God himself by attempting to put him in contradiction with himself in his kindhearted design. This was the deepest motive of the tempter from the beginning, when he became the Accuser of man before God, in an attempt to somehow make God despair of his own project of love.

The "opportune time" for this temptation begins on the evening of the Last Supper, on Holy Thursday: "Then Satan entered into Judas called

Iscariot, who was one of the twelve" (Luke 22:3). Satan no longer seeks to tempt Jesus directly; he will tempt him through someone who is dear to him. Several times Jesus said, "The Father does not want me to lose any of those he gave me." Those he has given him include all men; but these are represented in a very special way by the twelve, who constitute the nucleus of Jesus's family of disciples. Now it is precisely one of those whom Jesus has received from the Father that Satan tempts to the point of entering into him.

The entire episode that follows takes place on Holy Thursday evening, starting from this first moment when Satan enters into Judas and ending when Judas comes to arrest Jesus with the soldiers in Gethsemane. When Jesus arrives at Gethsemane with the three apostles, Peter, James, and John, he says to them, "Pray that you may not come into the time of trial" (Luke 22:40). And when Judas emerges, he exclaims, "But this is your hour, and the power of darkness!" (Luke 22:53), designating the darkness to which Judas has totally abandoned himself. Saint John indicates this very succinctly when he writes, "He [Judas] immediately went out. And it was night" (John 13:30).

And thus the hour of darkness has come. It is the "opportune time" when the Lamb can be hit full-on with the contradiction of created liberty (that of Satan first of all but also that of man, represented here by Judas, whom Satan has drawn into his own revolt). We are not confronted here, as we were in the episode when Christ was tempted in the desert, with temptation concerning a human matter. Jesus is now no longer tempted in his human weakness but in his divinity, because the Father's loving design that he carries within himself as the Lamb is about to be totally contradicted and apparently defeated by a created liberty that Christ came to redeem. This liberty belongs to Judas, as well as to all those who will make themselves the sons of perdition and who can render vain for themselves the Redemption itself.

The Rejection of God's Gift

To understand the mystery of Christ's "cup" at Gethsemane, the cup in which everything is going to converge, we must grasp the link that the gospel writers underline between the moment when Judas succumbs to the temptation of Satan and the mystery of the Eucharist. Saint John in particular states that Judas decides to betray Jesus at the very moment when Jesus gives him a morsel of bread during the Last Supper: "So he [Jesus] dipped the morsel and [took it and] handed it to Judas, son of Simon then Iscariot. After he took the morsel, Satan entered him" (John 13:26–27 NABRE). The "morsel" spoken of here can very well be the eucharistic bread that Jesus broke for his disciples at the start of the meal, before the announcement of the betrayal of Judas. This seems to be what Saint Luke suggests in his narrative of the Last Supper. Judas left before Jesus had completed the mystery of the new covenant in the cup of his blood. During the meal, Jesus began the eucharistic gesture by giving a morsel to Judas, thus fulfilling the psalm verse: "Even my bosom friend in whom I trusted, who ate of my bread, has lifted the heel against me" (Ps. 41:9). Jesus made this clear to Judas at the Last Supper, as he would do once again for the last time at Gethsemane, calling him "my friend" (Matt. 26:50).

The decision to betray Jesus is taken by Judas when he receives from the hands of the Lord the morsel of eucharistic bread; shortly afterward, he betrays the Lord by the sign of a kiss. In both instances, signs of eucharistic communion are brought into play. (The kiss of peace, it must be remembered, was a eucharistic sign dating to the apostolic church.) With the betrayal of Judas, these eucharistic signs are perverted because the grace that God gives through the innocence of the Lamb is turned against him by the contradiction of a refusal. All this is the work of Satan; it is his supreme temptation against God.

The eucharistic element, therefore, plays a very important role here: after receiving the morsel of broken bread, Judas departs; he excludes himself from the completion of the Eucharist in the final blessing of the cup of the covenant in the Lord's blood. Another text of Saint John indicates that Judas already began to close his heart to the mystery of Christ when he was confronted with the first revelations of the eucharistic mystery. John tells us that after having multiplied the loaves of bread, Jesus taught at length in the synagogue of Capernaum concerning the Bread of Life. He goes on to say:

> When many of his disciples heard it, they said, "This teaching is difficult; who can accept it?" But Jesus, being aware that his disciples were complaining about it, said to them, "Does this offend you? Then what if you were to see the Son of Man ascending to where he was before?

It is the spirit that gives life; the flesh is useless. The words that I have spoken to you are spirit and life. But among you there are some who do not believe." For Jesus knew from the first who were the ones that did not believe, and who was the one that would betray him. (John 6:60–64)

Saint John says that Jesus knew who it was who would betray him but not in the sense that Jesus anticipates the free decision of Judas. On the contrary, right up until the last moment, at the Last Supper, Jesus presents to this disciple a morsel of eucharistic bread, and in the Garden of Olives he calls him "my friend." Up until the last moment Judas is free, and God pursues him with his love until the end. But at Capernaum, Christ sees the origin of the closing of Judas's heart in his refusal of the Bread of Life: such a refusal is indeed characteristic of the refusal of a sacrificial Messiah, of a Messiah who gives his life.

This first perception of Judas's heart is indicated by Saint John in his conclusion of the Bread of Life episode: "Jesus asked the twelve, 'Do you also wish to go away?' Simon Peter answered him, 'Lord, to whom can we go? You have the words of eternal life. We have come to believe and know that you are the Holy One of God.' Jesus answered them, 'Did I not choose you, the twelve? Yet one of you is a devil.' He was speaking of Judas son of Simon Iscariot, for he, though one of the twelve, was going to betray him" (John 6:67–71).

One may wonder what Jesus saw in the heart of Judas. Could it perhaps have been the first idea of betrayal that crossed Judas's mind at the time of the Bread of Life discourse? This thought later gave rise to Judas's final decision of betrayal, at the moment when Jesus fulfilled the promise of the Bread of Life discourse by breaking the eucharistic bread at the Last Supper.

The refusal to recognize the body of the Lamb, offered in sacrifice, the refusal to be loved by God until the end, the demonic contradiction by which a person can exclude himself from God's love, all this leads us to another text, written this time by Saint Paul. After speaking of the eucharistic meal, Paul adds, "Examine yourselves, and only then eat of the bread and drink of the cup. For all who eat and drink without discerning the body, eat and drink judgment against themselves" (1 Cor. 11:28–29). The mystery of Judas's iniquity was perhaps an accomplishment of these words.

Judas approached Jesus as one of the twelve; he approached the mystery of the gift of his body, the total gift of God to men offered in an infinite love, but he refused this gift, and therefore the devil entered him with the morsel of eucharistic bread. He had communed with the entire being of the Incarnate Word, participating over a period of several years in every moment of his life, but he did so with an increasing resistance in his heart.

And thus we begin to perceive the link between the Eucharist (i.e., the gift of the Lamb) and the cup mentioned by Christ at Gethsemane. God has always given himself totally; he has always given himself entirely through grace to men, in his design to adopt them in his Son. But now he gives himself again in the Son who has become man, he gives himself as food, so that he can become, in man, the source of a re-creation that will cure him from his evils. But even this gift of himself, the blood that Christ sheds and in which he makes a complete offering of his love for men, can be received by a person for his own perdition.

Christ's blood is received in a cup: "This is the *cup* of my blood," says Jesus at the Last Supper. Jesus does not back away from the shedding of his blood as a total offering; he does not back away because his blood must necessarily be received in a cup: in the cup of man's liberty. He has come to save this liberty. But because it is free, this liberty is capable of contradicting salvation itself. Thus what Jesus refers to as the "hour of darkness" (see Luke 22:53) is situated between two distinct moments in time: the hour begins at the moment when Judas, receiving Christ's offered body, opens his heart to Satan and goes out into the night; it ends when he actually accomplishes his evil plan, handing Jesus over to his enemies by a kiss of betrayal at Gethsemane. The institution of the Eucharist and Christ's prayer of Gethsemane are like the two symmetrical panels of this mystery.

A Love Stronger Than Death

Jesus is the Son of God who has come in the flesh, in a human nature like unto our own but free from all sin. This human nature, because it is assumed by the divine person of the only begotten Son, does not constitute an autonomous human subject. This nature, innocent and totally united to a divine person, could not, in itself, be destined to die. Death, which all of us sense as a kind of contradiction of our natural desire to live, could only be all the more repugnant to Christ's human nature, which was free from sin and united to the "Prince of life." The dread that we experience in relation to death can hardly be compared to the revulsion that Jesus must have felt. In our case death is already gnawing at us from all sides; it is an inevitable consequence of our sin, the "wages of sin" (Rom. 6:23). As Augustine remarks, when we come into this life we are already beginning to die. Although we are terrified by death, we are in complicity with it because of our sin; death is not entirely foreign to us. Our whole life is an experience of death by sin and by all the forms of deprivation in our nature that accompany sin.

In the case of Jesus, the "form of a slave" doomed to die that he took upon himself from the beginning of his earthly life does violence to his human nature, first of all because his nature is sinless but second, and above all, because it is united in the person of the Prince of life, to the very life of God. Jesus's mortal condition is already a first sign of the contradiction of evil. Jesus must accept death in obedience to his divine will but as something that does violence to the most legitimate aspiration of his own human nature, which, more than that of any other man, was united with the divine life and thus made for life, not for death.

We see this in Saint John when Jesus enters Jerusalem. At that time, the hour is coming when all is to be accomplished, the hour when the Son of man will give his life. At that moment his soul is troubled: "Now my soul is troubled. And what should I say—'Father, save me from this hour?' No, it is for this reason that I have come to this hour. Father, glorify your name" (John 12:27–28).

Here we can perceive two registers or levels of expression. On the one hand, there is the spontaneous desire of Jesus's human nature, which senses a repugnance for a death that is infinitely more unnatural to him than to us, since he has no complicity with evil. Jesus expresses this natural desire in the words, "my soul is troubled . . . save me from this hour." On the other hand, Christ's divine will, which supports his human will, inspiring his human will's profoundest desire, is expressed in the words, "it is for this reason that I have come to this hour." This is a fulfillment of another passage of Saint John's gospel where Jesus says, "I have come down from heaven, not to do my will, but to do the will of him who sent me" (John 6:38). The entire human will of Jesus is the instrument of the mission of salvation that the Son received when he was sent in our human flesh by the Father.

The Son of God made man, by accepting the suffering and the death that are completely foreign to his nature, takes hold of the entire contradiction of evil that flouts divine love. The contradiction of evil against the eternal design of the Lamb, wounded by sin, is now manifested on the human level. Although the human nature of Jesus adds nothing to the love of God for us, God wants to reveal to us, in the suffering of the human nature that he has taken in the person of his Son, the impact in this created nature of his divine love flouted by our sin. The victorious assumption of evil involves, for the human will of Christ, accepting to offer up his life, even though his human nature was not made for death. His acceptance of this death is thus the created resonance of the assumption of the contradiction of our sin by God in his love. It adds nothing to this assumption but allows us to understand it, expressing it in terms of loss and human suffering.

The need to accept his death was after all something that Jesus took for granted. While Jesus gave expression to his natural desire to live by crying out and saying, "Now my soul is troubled. And what should I say—'Father, save me from this hour?'" he immediately continued, "No, it is for this reason that I have come to this hour. Father, glorify your name." These last words are an echo of the deepest commitment of his human will, which exists only for the mission of salvation entrusted to the Son by the Father. It is as if he had said, "Father, accomplish your design so as to manifest yourself as the Father." Not only is there no hesitation, no temptation in the human sense of the word, which would have involved a vacillation between a "yes" and a "no," but it is the deepest purpose of God that is expressed through the human will of Christ. "It is for this reason that I have come to this hour." It is as if he were saying, "My humanity does not have any mission other than to arrive at this hour. This hour of death, which is a pure contradiction of my humanity, is in fact the very meaning of my humanity, since I was born to human life in order to give my life for the salvation of the world." In this sense it does not seem that we can say that Christ was tempted to refuse the gift of his life. The test only begins when Satan enters into the heart of Judas with the morsel of eucharistic bread at the Last Supper.

The Hand-to-Hand Combat with Our Refusal

Jesus, in celebrating the Eucharist, already gives his life: "Take this all of you and eat of it, this is my body which is given up for you. Take this all of you and drink from it, for this is the cup of my blood which is poured out for you, the blood of the new covenant" (see Luke 22:19–20). Here Jesus seems to be calmly considering the gift of his life: "No one takes it [my life] from me, but I lay it down of my own accord. I have the power to lay it down, and I have the power to take it up again" (John 10:18). The contradiction that Jesus will encounter is at the heart of his eucharistic gift. It resides in a person who receives it: it is the mystery of the "cup." It manifests itself as soon as Jesus leaves the upper room with his disciples and when he himself enters into the night into which Judas has entered. At Gethsemane the same eucharistic reality of the gift of Christ's life for the salvation of the world is reproduced but in the night of the heart of Judas and of all those who do not want to receive this gift for their salvation. It is repeated at Gethsemane for those who can render vain in themselves the salvation that is offered to them by the Lamb.

"When he reached the place, he said to them, 'Pray that you may not come into the time of trial'" (Luke 22:40). Jesus senses the fragility of the human heart. Even Peter, James, and John will enter into temptation: they will fall asleep. Then all the apostles will be sifted, as Jesus had said to Peter, "Simon, Simon, listen! Satan has demanded to sift all of you like wheat, but I have prayed for you that your own faith may not fail; and you, when once you have turned back, strengthen your brothers" (Luke 22:31–32). Jesus is now confronted with the liberty of those who will receive salvation and who are pursued by the love of God who "loves them to the end" but always within that liberty itself that can never be canceled or bypassed.

"He took with him Peter and the two sons of Zebedee, and began to be grieved and agitated" (Matt. 26:37). This indication is very striking: "he *began* to be grieved and agitated." This is proof that during the institution of the Eucharist where Christ offered his life he did not experience any sorrow or distress. But the contradiction now hangs on the possible failure of this gift of life, the gift of his blood, in the person who receives it, that is, in the "cup" that receives it. It is not the sacrificing of his life that causes him distress, as was the case when he entered Jerusalem, but the fact that this gift of his life might not communicate life, or rather that the life it communicates might be smothered by the dark side of our liberty.

Then he said to them, "My soul is sorrowful even to death" (Matt. 26:38 NABRE). The death he mentions here is different from the one he spoke of earlier at the Last Supper. It is no longer a question of physical death: "*My soul* is sorrowful even to death." He is "dying of sorrow." Such is, in Jesus's created nature, the impact of God's uncreated love for men, which is contradicted by our sins: the sorrow that Jesus experiences is almost unbearable for him as a man, and his human nature collapses under so heavy an emotional weight. "And going a little farther, he threw himself on the ground" (Matt. 26:39). This is the prayer of someone who is crushed. Luke says he prayed on bent knee (Luke 22:41), an unusual position for Jesus to pray in as he usually addressed his prayers to the Father while standing. In this prayer, he expresses the terrible pressure exerted by those who contradict divine love, a pressure that causes his humanity to "fall to pieces": "In his anguish he prayed more earnestly, and his sweat became like great drops of blood falling down onto the ground" (Luke 22:44).

The Agony of Innocent Love

Christ's agony is a combat with death, with the death of sorrow. It is a struggle in which the divine innocence, God's obstinate love of man, can virtually be "put to death," rendered useless and defeated in those creatures who receive it with a liberty that has turned to evil. It is not the prospect of physical death that causes the agony of Jesus but the possible futility of his death in those for whom he is offering himself. The humanity of Jesus reaches a threshold of anguish and agony that is not comparable either to the loving tenderness of the Last Supper where he gave his life or to his serenity in suffering during the Passion on the cross. In Christ's life, the agony constitutes a specific and unique event that is closely related to the "mystery of Judas." It begins when Jesus enters into the night into which Judas entered, and it ends at the moment when Judas kisses Jesus. Between the eucharistic morsel through which Satan enters into Judas and the treacherous kiss by which Judas refuses the love of the God who is the

"Friend of men," a mysterious night unfolds that coincides with the night of the sin of the world, and with the liberty of each of us for whom this night can ultimately lead to eternal damnation.

Christ expresses his agony in a dialogue with the Father. This dialogue with the Father has a fundamentally important feature in the Gospel according to Mark: here for first time Jesus addresses God as "Abba." It is in the dialogue of the agony that this word is revealed to us as the ultimate way of designating divine fatherhood: "He said, 'Abba, Father [the Aramaic word *Abba*, which means "Daddy," was incorporated into the original Greek text], for you all things are possible; remove this cup from me; yet, not what I want, but what you want" (Mark 14:36). There is an intrinsic link between the revelation of God as "Abba" and the mystery of the cup. The mystery of the cup represents the supreme contradiction constituted not by the Lord's death but by the damnation of men that can cancel the redemptive effect of Christ's death itself. Jesus addresses the Father, for he knows that it is he who is presenting this cup to him. That is why he concludes his request by saying, "Yet, not what I want, but what you want." In the unique rhythm of this prayer, Jesus expresses the very essence of the divine will of the Father that the Son makes his own, from all eternity, in the Amen of the Lamb. God's design to give man divine sonship through grace necessarily implies human liberty and therefore also the ambivalence of the cup. The cup cannot be removed, for it is there that the blood of the atoning sacrifice must be received. God must pour his love into the liberty of man; he cannot pour his grace anywhere other than into this liberty, because he is offering a grace of sonship that is intended to animate human liberty, arousing a response but without ever suppressing that liberty.

Coming out of this dialogue with the Father at the end of his agony, when Judas comes to arrest him with the soldiers and when Peter wants to defend him with the sword, Jesus says to Peter, "Put your sword back into its sheath. Am I not to drink the cup that the Father has given me?" (John 18:11). Because the cup is given by "Abba," because it expresses the very heart of "Abba," Jesus accepts the supreme contradiction of the kiss of Judas. As was the case with the morsel of bread at the Last Supper, the kiss of peace, sign of communion and love, also becomes at Gethsemane a sign of betrayal and of the turning of grace against its source in God.

The mystery of the cup is revealed in a passage of the Epistle to the Hebrews: "Let us run with perseverance the race that is set before us, looking to Jesus the pioneer and perfecter of our faith, who for the sake of the joy that was set before him endured the cross, disregarding its shame, and has taken his seat at the right hand of the throne of God. Consider him who endured such hostility against himself from sinners" (Heb. 12:1–3). The Greek word *antilogia* is very strong because it designates a contradiction against the very heart of the Word, that is, against the "Logos" who expresses God's design. The contradiction of sin seeks to turn the design of grace against itself.

The Darkness of Contradiction

"Consider him who endured such hostility against himself from sinners, so that you may not grow weary or lose heart" (Heb. 12:3). "My soul is sorrowful even to death," said Jesus (Matt. 26:38 NABRE). Experiencing this contradiction involves a confrontation with the "sin against the Holy Spirit." It occurs when the love that is being offered is received in a "cup" that refuses and negates it in itself. This caused Jesus to experience fatigue of the soul, sorrow, agony, a sense of powerlessness at the very moment when he was offering the total gift of salvation. The author of Hebrews points to Jesus's way of enduring contradiction as an example for us to follow: "In the struggle against sin you have not yet resisted to the point of shedding your blood" (Heb. 12:4). Jesus offers his life in the seemingly "mad" dynamics of a love that does not take into account the possibility that it will be contradicted by a refusal. It is the blind love that appears in the Fra Angelico icon, on the morning of Good Friday, when the God of Love, blindfolded, receives the contradiction of evil in full force, like a slap in the face.

Paradoxically, love "sees" this contradiction in the night. In this nocturnal temptation, Satan takes God to the place where he wanted to bring him: he confronts God with the refusal of man; he confronts him with the "divine temptation." "You shall not tempt the Lord your God" (Luke 4:12 NKJV): by this phrase, which concludes (in Luke's gospel) the third temptation in the desert, Jesus obliges Satan to fall back no longer on merely human temptations but on the ultimate divine temptation: that of showing God the failure of his kindhearted design because of the definitive and radical "no" by which a created liberty can refuse it. Satan submits the Son of God precisely to this temptation during the night of Gethsemane. He does this through Judas, as well as through all those whom Judas represents. It is now that Satan causes Jesus to look into the darkness, and it is this that constitutes the "hour of darkness": the following day, Good Friday, there will no longer be any "agony" because the divine love, in the Lamb who bears our sins, will already in the agony of Gethsemane have persevered in love through the darkness itself. Just as the love of the creator, in conceiving his design, did not take into account the possibility of a negative response on the part of man, the love of the Redeemer will likewise persevere in love without considering that a refusal is always possible. This love will go forward blindfolded, through the contradiction of evil.

At Gethsemane, however, in the hour of darkness and of the supreme temptation, the Lord is confronted with evil. In the Eastern iconographic tradition, the icon of Christ's temptation in the Garden is called "the icon of Christ whose eyes do not sleep." The title alludes to the fact that Jesus remained awake and vigilant throughout the entire night of the agony and that he said to the apostles, "Get up and pray that you may not come into the time of trial" (Luke 22:46). These "eyes that do not sleep" are eyes that were confronted with the contradiction of love by the darkness of sin. This is what causes the "agony," which, lest we forget it, means first of all, "struggle." Christ will take hold of the contradiction of sin by loving sinners "until the end," even through the possibility that this love may be eternally refused and rejected. Christ wants to love forever even the person who has set himself forever in such a refusal. Jesus's agony is entirely caused by the anxiety of having to shed his blood in a cup of blessing and redemption that the liberty of man can turn into a cup of wrath and eternal damnation.

The Tempter of God

But before tackling directly the mystery of the cup, I must say something about the tempter, the one who is going to present the cup, the tempter who insists on showing the darkness to the One who is the light, the tempter who wants to force the love of the creator to look with open eyes on the possibility of a refusal. The book of Job already shows us how this tempter dares to tempt God himself.

> One day the heavenly beings came to present themselves before the Lord, and Satan also came among them. The Lord said to Satan, "Where have you come from?" Satan answered the Lord, "From going to and fro on the earth, and walking up and down on it." The Lord said to Satan, "Have you considered my servant Job? There is no one like him on earth, a blameless and upright man who fears God and turns away from evil." Then Satan answered the Lord, "Does Job fear God for nothing? Have you not put a fence around him and his house and all that he has, on every side? You have blessed the work of his hands, and his possessions have increased in the land. But stretch out your hand now, and touch all that he has, and he will curse you to your face." The Lord said to Satan, "Very well, all that he has is in your power; only do not stretch out your hand against him!" (Job 1:6–12)

Having destroyed Job's property and killed his children, Satan appears again before God, who says, "'Have you considered my servant Job? There is no one like him on the earth, a blameless and upright man who fears God and turns away from evil. He still persists in his integrity, although you incited me against him, to destroy him for no reason.' Then Satan answered the Lord, 'Skin for skin! All that people have they will give to save their lives. But stretch out your hand now and touch his bone and his flesh, and he will curse you to your face.' The Lord said to Satan, 'Very well, he is in your power; only spare his life'" (Job 2:3–6). Satan is the enemy of man, the adversary, "a murderer from the beginning" (John 8:44). He is the one who accuses men before God (Rev. 12:10). His role throughout the prologue of the book of Job is to cause God to despair concerning man and to repent over the purpose of adoption that he willed for him.

Satan's temptation is twofold. He begins by tempting man in order to cause man to say "no" to God. He then tries to tempt God concerning man by saying to the Lord, "You see, man does not respond to your love. Your kindhearted design is in vain." In the prophet Zechariah Satan also appears: "Then he [the man] showed me the high priest Joshua standing before the angel of the Lord, and Satan standing at his right hand to accuse him" (Zech. 3:1). Joshua the high priest represents Israel. He is dressed in dirty clothes when he stands before the angel of the Lord: he is carrying sins, as the high priest bore the sins of Israel at the time of Yom Kippur, when he invoked the name of God for the forgiveness of all the sins of the people. But Satan stands before God as the accuser, that is, to show God the sins of man. But the angel of the Lord awaits the victory of God's love, and he says to Satan, "The Lord rebuke you, O Satan! The Lord who has chosen Jerusalem rebuke you" (Zech. 3:2).

The angel of the Lord, who will appear later in the book of Daniel as the archangel Michael, responds here by invoking the name of God and by mentioning the purpose of God who has chosen Jerusalem. He refutes Satan's accusation by making him sense that the loving design of God is stronger than his accusation, which will be rejected by the Lord. We have echoes of this in the Epistle of Saint Jude: "When the archangel Michael contended with the devil and disputed about the body of Moses, he did not dare to bring a condemnation of slander against him, but said, 'The Lord rebuke you'" (Jude 1:9). Here reference is made to the text of an apocryphal writing, an apocalypse titled the Assumption of Moses. In the desert Moses sinned together with the people, and, like the entire generation of those who left Egypt, he could not enter the Promised Land. This apocalyptic text shows Satan raising a dispute over his body. This is very mysterious since Moses had no tomb; he died on Mount Nebo, and no one knew where he was buried. This apocalyptic text, immediately prior to Jesus, gives the impression that there was a dispute about all this, with Satan accusing Moses before God for a lack of faith and the archangel Michael (the angel of the Lord who protects the people of God) snatching from the devil Moses's body, claiming for God, as it were, that which rightfully belongs to him and repelling Satan with the same words from the book of Zechariah: "May the Lord rebuke you."

Satan poses himself as the accuser of man before God because, as the book of Wisdom says, he is jealous: "Through the devil's envy death entered the world" (Wis. 2:24). For this reason he is a "murderer from the beginning": he wants to prove to God that his purpose for man, his design of adoption, is folly. He is also the "enemy" who sows tares in the field of God, according to Christ's parable: "The enemy who sowed them is the devil" (Matt. 13:39). These tares are precisely the contradiction of ill will or of sin.

CHAPTER NINE

The Mysterious Ambivalence of the Cup

The temptation of Gethsemane is the supreme and ultimate temptation that the devil presents to God in relation to his kindhearted design for the adoption of men. It is in the form of the cup that this temptation appears. This cup is essentially the cup of salvation; however, throughout the literature of the Old Testament, it can also become the cup of wrath and malediction. Through the symbol of the cup is expressed all the ambivalence of liberty that constitutes the vulnerable aspect of God's design as the mystery of the Lamb. The contradiction "inflicted" on the Lord by Satan and by those whom he entices to follow him resides in the fact that grace can be turned against its own source in God by the liberty of those who receive it.

The Cup: A Blessing of Liberty

The mystery of the cup is the mystery of a blessing that the liberty of a person can turn into a curse for his doom. It seems that the ambiguity of the cup is revealed in the fact that in ancient times it was used to draw lots. Pieces of dice were probably put in a cup and shaken in order to draw lots. In Psalm 16 we read, "The Lord is my chosen portion and my cup; you who hold my lot. The boundary lines have fallen for me in pleasant places; I have a goodly heritage" (Ps. 16:5–6). It is very curious to note that the lot of the inheritance can be expressed by the cup. The Levites had no inheritance in Israel, while every other tribe had its portion of territory. Psalm 16 is the song of the Levites who have no inheritance because the cup has assigned to them God himself as their inheritance. The cup used for the drawing of lots assigned to the Levites the possession of a lot that is nothing other than God himself. And thus the cup takes on the meaning of a "cup of blessing."

> You prepare a table before me
> in the presence of my enemies;
> you anoint my head with oil;
> my cup overflows.
> (Ps. 23:5)

> What shall I return to the Lord
> for all his bounty to me?
> I will lift up the cup of salvation
> and call on the name of the Lord.
> (Ps. 116:12–13)

This positive meaning of the cup will be developed further in Judaism by the blessing pronounced over the cup of wine every Sabbath and at every festive meal. We see it in the Last Supper narrative of Saint Luke (Luke 22:17): The meal begins with a blessing of the cup that is not yet the eucharistic blessing. Indeed, Luke speaks of two cups. Over the first, thanks was given with the prayer formula that we now use in the offertory of Mass: "Blessed are you, Lord God of the all creation, for through your goodness we have received this wine we offer you, fruit of the vine." This prayer recognized that the blessing of God is most fully gathered in that which is the sign of abundance. While bread is something absolutely necessary for our sustenance, wine is not. It is instead the sign of a festival or celebration; it is a sign of a superabundance of love. This is why in Judaism a cup is blessed at marriages as the sign of the free gift of love. The cup overflows with "wine to gladden the human heart" (Ps. 104:15), as a pure gift from God. So, starting already with Judaism, the ultimate act of thanksgiving is accomplished during the blessing of the cup.

Paul tells the Corinthians, "The cup of blessing that we bless, is it not a sharing in the blood of Christ?" (1 Cor. 10:16). We have here the junction between the Eucharist and the Jewish blessing of the cup. At the Last Supper, Jesus, taking the cup, offered thanksgiving for the new and everlasting covenant: "Then he took a cup, and after giving thanks he gave it to them, saying, 'Drink from it, all of you; for this is my blood of the covenant, which is poured out for many for the forgiveness of sins'" (Matt. 26:27–28).

Into the cup Christ will pour his blood, that is, the sign of life, a superabundant and eternal life, and of a love that perseveres to the end. The eucharistic wine is the sacrament of blood, which in Judaism signifies the very life of the Spirit. Such is the gift that man receives in the Eucharist as a supreme blessing, the supreme proof of divine love.

The mystery of the Lamb is contained in the cup that receives his blood. This cup is first of all the cup of blessing in which God completely communicates his loving paternity through the beloved Son. This cup, however, also carries the possibility that its blessing may be transformed by us into a curse. This is so because the cup stands for our liberty, and God gives himself by proposing himself to us from within our liberty. To give himself to a person in any other way would not be a gift to a person's liberty but would instead destroy that liberty. But in his kindhearted design, God has immense respect for liberty. Such is the mystery of the Lamb, which I have designated as the vulnerability of God in relation to our liberty.

The Cup and the Drunkenness of Pride

It is therefore necessary now to explore the somber possibility of the cup of blessing being transformed into a cup of wrath. The contents of the cup help us understand its ambiguity: the wine, which is a sign of a superabundant blessing, can, nevertheless, turn the heads of men. Concerning the cup that makes men mad when they drink, the Old Testament offers us first an episode from Genesis, which tells us that "Noah, a man of the soil, was the first to plant a vineyard (this happens just after the flood).

> He drank some of the wine and became drunk, and he lay uncovered in his tent. And Ham, the father of Canaan, saw the nakedness of his father, and told his two brothers outside. Then Shem and Japheth took a garment, laid it on both their shoulders, and walked backward and covered the nakedness of their father; their faces were turned away, and they did not see their father's nakedness. When Noah awoke from his wine and knew what his youngest son had done to him, he said, "Cursed be Canaan [Ham]; lowest of slaves shall he be to his brothers." (Gen. 9:20–25)

The blessing, like wine, can intoxicate man. In his drunkenness man can go mad, imagining himself to be something more than what he really is. Excessive wine drinking can make his head dizzy and puffed up with pride. But it is precisely in this intoxication of his pride that man exposes his nakedness: just when he thinks of himself as someone big and important, his nothingness appears for his shame. All the Old Testament texts involving the cup are centered on this point. But far worse than those who intoxicate themselves is the one who gives the cup to others in order to make them drunk so that he can look on their nakedness and make fun of them. Such a person is even more reprehensible. The blessing becomes a curse for whoever gets drunk but even more for those who actively seek to intoxicate others.

The texts concerning the cup of wrath are quite numerous. I review them in roughly chronological order, taking into account the knowledge we have of their historical context. I should note that in the passages of the prophets that mention the cup, there are indirect allusions to the drunkenness of Noah in Genesis. The oldest text we have is perhaps this passage from Habakkuk, a prophet who is a contemporary of Jeremiah: "Alas for you who make your neighbors drink, pouring out your wrath until they are drunk, in order to gaze on their nakedness! You will be sated with contempt instead of glory. Drink, you yourself, and stagger! The cup in the Lord's right hand will come around to you, and shame will come upon your glory" (Hab. 2:15–16). In this very comprehensive text we find all the elements: the cup, wine, and drunkenness but above all the action of making others drink in order to get them drunk and look on their nakedness. This infamy, however, soon turns against the tempter himself: his turn comes to drink the cup, which the Lord foists upon him. The tempter who foisted the cup upon others is now himself obliged to drink and to show his infamy.

In the Lamentations of Jeremiah, this link is equally explicit:

> Rejoice and be glad, O daughter of Edom,
> you that live in the land of Uz;
> but to you also the cup shall pass;
> you shall become drunk and strip yourself bare.
> (Lam. 4:21)

The daughter of Edom designates the attackers of Jerusalem, the Babylonians, who became intoxicated by their victory and to whom Jeremiah said, "Get drunk yourselves, but in doing so you too will drink of this cup, and one day you will expose your own nakedness." It is always the same idea. The blessing that we have received can also be used for manipulation when we decide to seize the cup with our own hands. It that case, the blessing itself becomes a curse. As soon as we begin to appropriate grace for ourselves, we are already falling into drunkenness and we are on the way to showing our nakedness.

> But it is God who executes judgment, putting down one and
> lifting up another.
> For in the hand of the Lord there is a cup
> with foaming wine, well mixed;
> he will pour a draught from it,
> and all the wicked of the earth shall drain it down to the dregs.
> (Ps. 75:7–9)

Here the cup of drunkenness is in the hands of God, who humiliates some and raises up others. But it must be understood, in light of the previous texts, that it is the liberty of man who transforms the cup of blessing into a cup of drunkenness. The interesting reference to a "foaming wine" in the cup brings to mind the reproaches addressed to the apostles on Pentecost, "They are full of sweet wine." This sweet wine is precisely foaming wine, wine that is still in the process of fermentation and that therefore goes straight to the head. It is not the same thing as the "new wine" that is mentioned in the gospel, a wine that is already more stabilized. Whoever drinks of it feels exalted, but it soon becomes clear that he has in fact been drinking from the cup of God the Judge, and in the folly of his pride, he is thrown to the ground. Such are the vicissitudes of destiny. The combination of these various images depicts a dramatic reversal of situations, a change of lots in life. Pride is shown to be that which causes a person to be precipitated downward so that he inherits a curse instead of a blessing. We have here the exact opposite of the earlier mentioned idea of a cup being used to draw lots. Pride can cause the "delightful portion" intended for someone as the lot that is drawn from the cup to become instead a curse befitting the ungodly: "On the wicked he [God] will rain coals of fire and sulfur; a scorching wind shall be the portion of their cup" (Ps. 11:6).

Based on this principle, a long series of texts in Jeremiah presents the cup as the expression of divine malediction.

> You shall speak to them this word:
> Thus says the Lord, the God of Israel:
> Every wine-jar should be filled with wine.
> And they will say to you, "Do you think we do not know
> that every wine-jar should be filled with wine?"
> Then you shall say to them:
> Thus saith the Lord:
> I am about to fill all the inhabitants of this land—
> the kings who sit on David's throne,
> the priests, the prophets,
> and all the inhabitants of Jerusalem—with drunkenness.
> And I will dash them one against another,
> the parents and children together,
> says the Lord.
> I will not pity or spare or have any compassion
> when I destroy them.
>
> (Jer. 13:12–14)

Pride and intoxication, the source of perdition, are expressed here by the wine. The wine fills the jug of man's destiny; but when the jug is full of wine, and that wine is a wine of madness, God can only smash and break the jugs one against another.

The Cup of God's Wrath

> The Lord, God of Israel, said to me:
> Take from my hand this cup of the wine of wrath,
> and make all the nations to whom
> I send you drink it.
>
> (Jer. 25:15)

Here we see for the first time the expression "cup of the wine of wrath." It is very important to understand that this cup of wrath only became such because it was the cup in which man intoxicated himself with his own ego, with his own pride; otherwise one might think that the wrath of God is willed as such by the Lord himself. The wrath of God is never a feeling or passion that emanates from God's heart in the form of anger, even if sometimes the Bible presents things in a very anthropomorphic way. It is we ourselves who are the authors of God's wrath; it is his flouted love that, through us and for us, becomes wrath. It is not he who becomes angry: his cup contained only blessings. If in our drunkenness we derive from it a curse for ourselves, it is we who are the authors of the wrath that punishes us. It is interesting to note that the cup becomes a cup of wrath only for the person who gets drunk and exposes his nakedness, thus becoming the unique cause of his own downfall.

> Say to them, Thus says the Lord of Hosts, the God of Israel:
> Drink, get drunk and vomit, fall and rise no more,
> because of the sword that I am sending among you.
> And if they refuse to accept the cup from your hand to drink,
> then you shall say to them: Thus says the Lord of Hosts:
> > You must drink.
>
> (Jer. 25:27–28)

We have here some extremely anthropomorphic expressions of God's wrath. One could get the impression that God almost forces man to take the wrong direction. But, on the contrary, this is a Semitic way of expressing God's despair when he comes up against the contradiction of man's sin. When he says, "If they do not want to drink, tell them, you must drink!" he actually knows very well that they will drink and that they are obstinate. The words "drink, get drunk and vomit" are a simple observation of the facts that are presented, inexactly, as orders. God is obliged to take into account the consequences of human liberty, and he explodes with anger because he cannot resign himself to the unhappiness that results from it for man. Do parents sometimes not say things like this to their disobedient children: "Go ahead, fall if you must. . . . Good, you have fallen, now you see where you have ended up?" One could almost get the impression that they are rejoicing over the fact that their child has fallen or burned himself when in fact they are crying out with pain: "I told you so. You did not want to listen. You were absolutely bent on doing it!" The Bible is speaking here in a very human way to indicate a strongly sensitive parental reaction. This is what is indicated at the end of the Epistle to the Hebrews (12:5–13), where we find the key to the "wrath" of God. When God disciplines someone, this shows that he is treating him as his own son, not as an illegitimate child; he would not discipline someone whom he did not consider his child. Parents are personally wounded by anything that adversely affects their own children, and therefore they are very demanding with them. God proves that he is our Father precisely when he gets angry with us, because the sin that affects us touches him in his love. Wrath is nothing other than God's love itself, when he shudders to see how we rush toward evil and how we pervert his blessing for our own misfortune.

We are obliged to set things back in their proper perspective when reading certain biblical texts. It is always necessary to remember that the psalms of imprecation, the cries of anger in the Old Testament, and even the anger of Jesus are ways of expressing the nonacceptance of evil by God. At the very moment when the Lord takes it upon himself, he cannot tolerate or accept it in its principle; he cannot even conceive it. He is obliged to acknowledge the disastrous consequences of evil for his children while at the same time exploding with anger and interposing a radical and absolute "no." This is expressed in the passionate and sometimes very human language of Psalms ("dash their heads against the rocks"; "stab them, pierce them with the sword," etc.). But even if the psalmist is still unable to make a clear distinction between the sin and the sinners, he testifies to the holiness of God who cannot resign himself to evil. We are obliged to adopt and assimilate all the intermediate images through which this revelation is given, because it relates to the nonacceptance of evil by the Lamb himself who is assailed by it full-on. And precisely because he is hit by it in full force, he is able to take hold of it victoriously, by saying "no" even as he takes it upon himself; because in fact he does not accept the evil as such but the liberty that can cause evil, which is quite a different thing. God does not "permit" evil; he permits liberty that can cause the evil act. God does not permit drunkenness; he permits the freedom of the man who gets drunk.

The Cup of Self-Destruction

To correct what might be excessive in these angry shouts of God, we must remember this passage from Hosea: although God is angry with his people because of their infidelity (Hosea 11:1–11), he says: "How can I give you up, Ephraim.... My heart recoils within me; my compassion grows warm and tender" (Hosea 11:8). God is angry against the evil through which his creatures are destroying themselves. He is angry precisely because he loves them and wants to save them.

But the root of sin is always pride: "Make him drunk, because he magnified himself against the Lord; let Moab wallow in his vomit; he too shall become a laughingstock. Israel was a laughingstock for you, though he was not caught among thieves; but whenever you spoke of him you shook your head" (Jer. 48:26–27). Moab mocked Israel at the time of its misery. But now it is Moab's turn to roll in the vomit of his drunkenness and become the laughingstock of others. It really seems impossible to separate the two themes, pride and drunkenness.

"Babylon was a golden cup in the Lord's hand, making all the earth drunken; the nations drank her wine, and so the nations went mad. Suddenly Babylon has fallen and is shattered" (Jer. 51:7–8). Babylon, when she was powerful and strong, became intoxicated herself, and she intoxicated everyone around her; everyone was worshipping her power and might. Here we have the source of all the passages from the book of Revelation that speak of Babylon as the cup of God's wrath. "The great city was split into three parts, and the cities of the nations fell. God remembered great Babylon [i.e., Rome, the "Babylon" of the New Testament] and gave her the wine-cup of the fury of his wrath" (Rev. 16:19).

The idea of the cup filled with wine is reminiscent of the theme from Psalm 75, about sweet foaming wine that makes the head spin. And it is the intoxication of pride that causes the wrath of God.

Here now is a text from the prophet Isaiah: "Rouse yourself, rouse yourself! Stand up, O Jerusalem, you who have drunk at the hand of the Lord the cup of his wrath, who have drunk to the dregs the bowl of staggering" (Isa. 51:17).

The image of the cup that causes staggering continues the theme of drunkenness.

> There is none to guide her among all the children she has borne;
> there is no one to take her by the hand among all the children
>   she has brought up.
> These two things have befallen you — who will grieve with you? —
> devastation and destruction, famine and sword —
> who will comfort you?
> Your children have fainted, they lie at the head of every street
>   like an antelope in a net;
> they are full of the wrath of the Lord, the rebuke of your God.
> Therefore hear this, you who are wounded,
> who are drunk, but not with wine:
> Thus says your Sovereign, the Lord, your God who pleads
>   the cause of his people:
> See, I have taken from your hand the cup of staggering;
> you shall drink no more from the bowl of my wrath.
> And I will put it into the hand of your tormentors,
>   who have said to you,
> "Bow down, that we may walk on you";
> and you have made your back like the ground and like the street
>   for them to walk on.
>
> (Isa. 51:18–23)

God takes the cup away from Jerusalem, and it is now those who have oppressed her who must drink this same "staggering cup."

The same theme of the cup of wrath is found in the book of Revelation: "Those who worship the beast and its image, and receive a mark on their foreheads or on their hands, they will also drink the wine of God's wrath, poured unmixed into the cup of his anger, and they will be tormented with fire and sulfur in the presence of the holy angels and in the presence of the Lamb" (Rev. 14:9–10). This very important passage illustrates two things. First, the theme of the cup of wrath is quite present in the New Testament and is therefore the key for understanding the cup of Gethsemane. Second, the term "cup of wrath" had already taken on in the Christianity of the apostolic period the sense of eternal damnation. The expression, "They will be tormented with fire and sulfur in the presence of the holy angels and in the presence of the Lamb," signifies hell.

But before that, other references to the cup of wrath designate the misfortunes of history: "Then one of the four living creatures gave the seven angels seven golden bowls full of the wrath of God" (Rev. 15:7). And further on: "I heard a loud voice from the temple telling the seven angels, 'Go and pour out on the earth the seven bowls of the wrath of God'" (Rev. 16:1). This passage, where God is said to actually pour out his wrath, would seem scandalous if we were to take the theme of the cup of wrath in the book of Revelation without considering its origins in the Old Testament. If we did not recall the theme of drunkenness in the Old Testament, where the cup, which is in itself a blessing, can be changed into a curse by the drunkenness of pride that causes men to stagger and lose their heads, we would probably even fail to notice that in Revelation, God's wrath is said to be contained in a *cup*.

Here are two final Old Testament echoes of the theme of the cup, found in the more recent minor prophets.

> For as you have drunk on my holy mountain,
> all nations around you shall drink;
> they shall drink and gulp down,
> and shall be as though they had never been.
>
> (Obad. 1:16)

When those who have gotten drunk and gorged themselves awaken, they come out of a nightmare that is pure delirium. Such is the hallucination of evil, which has no being or existence in itself. If we become puffed up with pride, our nothingness appears in all its nakedness.

"See, I am about to make Jerusalem a cup of reeling for all the surrounding peoples [during] the siege against Jerusalem" (Zech. 12:2). Why has Jerusalem become a cup? Because all the other peoples, seeing her weakness, will become proud when taking advantage of her. At that time Jerusalem, which they hold in their hands, becomes for them instead a stumbling block. Once again we have the same reversal: this is the deepest insight into the mystery of evil, and it runs through the entire Old Testament.

Jesus expressed the mystery of his Passion by the image of the cup in his response to the request of the mother of the two sons of Zebedee: "You do not know what you are asking" (Matt. 20:22; Mark 10:38). The two disciples are as if "drunk." They ask through their mother to sit on the right or the left of Jesus. It is very striking to note how their heads were spinning on that day when they asked the Lord for the first two places in his kingdom. Jesus's answer shows them their folly: "You do not know what you are asking!"

And Jesus adds, "Are you able to drink the cup that I drink, or to be baptized with the baptism that I am baptized with?" And they say to him (still in their "drunkenness"), "We are able." But Jesus says, "The cup that I drink you will drink; and with the baptism with which I am baptized, you will be baptized" (but only later). "But to sit at my right hand or at my left is not mine to grant" (Mark 10:38–40). The cup is here related to baptism. It expresses above all a test or a trial. Jesus mentions the cup to these apostles who are in the very typical condition of spiritual drunkenness that causes their heads to spin.

This study of the biblical meaning of the cup helps us understand the prayer of Gethsemane and the mystery of Christ's agony. The love of God contained in the eucharistic cup of the Last Supper, through the gift of life that Jesus offers for the salvation of the multitude, must be received in the cup of human liberty. However, this superabundant, incomparable blessing can itself become an occasion of folly and pride. Did not Judas betray the Lord out of disappointment, because Jesus turned out not to be the triumphant Messiah he had been expecting? Did not the demon begin to enter into Judas's heart during the Bread of Life discourse, precisely because Jesus spoke a language this disciple found hard to bear, a language announcing Christ's sacrifice for the life of the world (John 6:64–70)? And the devil, did he not enter Judas with the morsel of eucharistic bread that Jesus had broken and given to him (John 13:27; Luke 22:21)?

CHAPTER TEN

In the Cell of Mercy

At Gethsemane Jesus goes into agony because his human nature has become like the focal point where the love of God meets and takes up into itself the ultimate contradiction, represented by the possibility that created liberty has to incur damnation. It is this contradiction that wounded the Lamb, from the very moment when, in the folly of pride, original sin was committed, after the serpent tempted the first couple, saying, "You shall be as gods." Jesus's humanity is entirely dislocated as a result of this contradiction. His disarray at Gethsemane no longer stems from the mere fact that he must give his life; it is no longer the simple fear of death, as seems to have been the case earlier when Jesus was entering Jerusalem (John 12:27). Indeed, this fear of death was quite natural, and in the case of the Lord it was even more than natural, since, as noted above, Jesus's sinless nature was fully united to the person of the Son of God himself, who is the "Author of life" (Acts 3:15). But at Gethsemane, the Lord's agony involves hand-to-hand combat with evil as such, with the ill will of human liberty that says "no" to God and that therefore causes the Redemption, for which Christ is offering his life, to appear hopelessly ridiculous and ineffective. At Gethsemane, we can almost hear the ironic laughter of Satan. In the cup of created liberty, Satan associates his own ill will with that of Judas. The devil insists on confronting God, at the very moment when his incarnate Son is offering his love unto the end, with the resolute "no" by which a man can stand in opposition to the Lord, causing the divine plan of salvation to fail by choosing instead his own damnation.

The Cup of God's Desire

From here on in, it might be good for greater certitude to base my discussion on the words of Saint Catherine of Siena. The mystery evoked here is so profound that we would do well to hold the hand of a saint whom God has introduced into the cell of mercy of his fatherly heart. Saint Catherine prayed very often at night. Following the example of her father, Saint Dominic, she felt called to spend the greater part of her nights in prayer. In her cell in the course of those nights, Saint Catherine can focus our gaze on Jesus during his night at Gethsemane. Here is how she explains, according to the revelations she received from Christ himself, the mystery of that night. Although she was without our present-day biblical expertise, her exquisite supernatural intuitions enabled her to touch on the very heart of this mystery, and she was able to express it better than anyone can today.

"She gave," wrote her biographer and spiritual father, the Blessed Raymond of Capua,

> an explanation of the words of Our Lord in the Garden of Olives, which I do not recall having read or heard anywhere else. She maintained that persons who have been enlightened and fortified by grace should not believe, as weaker souls, who fear death, do, that the Savior was asking to be delivered from his Passion when he said: "Father, let this cup pass away from me" (Mt. 26:39). Indeed, he had been drinking ever since his birth, and as the end approached, he was drinking more and more from this *cup of the desire to save all men* [translator's emphasis]. In his prayer at Gethsemane, he was really asking for the full achievement or completion of that which he so ardently desired. He would have liked to immediately finish off this chalice whose bitterness he

had already been enduring for so long. . . . But though this cup of desire was very painful for him to drink, he prayed in his filial obedience saying: "however, let not my will, but yours be done" (Lk. 22:42). In this way he offered to endure all the delays it would please the Father to bring in the accomplishment of his Passion.

The agony of Gethsemane is the contradiction of God's desire to bring salvation, a contradiction stemming from the delays and failures imposed on the divine plan by those with rebellious free wills. "The desire of the Son of God," writes Saint Catherine,

> was his hunger for our salvation, in order to accomplish the will of his Father; this is what caused him to suffer until he had accomplished it. And because he is the Wisdom of the Father, he saw those who would benefit from the blood he shed for them, and those who would not benefit from it, through their own fault, and he was crying bitterly over the blindness of those who do not want to profit from it. He actually suffered this torment of desire from his birth right up until his death. Then, after he had given his life, the torment, the cross of desire, ceased, but not the desire itself.

What immediately strikes us here is that Saint Catherine speaks of a vision of Christ that makes him contemporary to everyone in the exercise of their liberty, to those benefiting and those not benefiting from his redeeming blood. Let us note that this has nothing to do with a prevision or a foretelling of the future that would imply predestination in the order of evil. Instead Christ carries our liberty in the present moment of our acts, a moment coinciding with the present moment of God's eternity.

In Agony until the End of the World

In the cup of Gethsemane all our free-will decisions, from the beginning of time until the end, are gathered together in God's eternal present moment. For the Lamb has been "slain since the beginning of the world," and Christ, as Pascal says, "remains in agony until the end of time." Saint

Catherine's biographer continues, reporting that during one of her ecstasies she declared, "That which caused the Savior to experience such great sadness and to sweat blood at Gethsemane, was the sight of so many souls who would not participate in the fruits of his Passion." The agony is in the hour of darkness the expression, in Christ's human nature, of the contradiction against God's eternal Love, arising from the evil acts committed by our free wills in present time.

"The precious blood of my only begotten Son," says God to Saint Catherine in the *Dialogue*, "destroyed death, dispelled the darkness, diffused light; that blood continually works for the salvation and perfection of the man who disposes himself to receive it. But just as it gives life, it can also give death to the one who drinks unworthily in the darkness of sin. Yes indeed, the sinner acts cruelly against himself when he tramples in his heart, the fruit of the precious Blood." This is the Savior's agony, accepting from the hand of the Father that his blood be collected in the cup, that is, in the free will of man. "We ourselves stand here as cups," said Saint Catherine, "ready to receive the blood that flowed from the Cross. It is we who are the cup that receives his blood." When Jesus said, "Father, let this cup pass from me," we ought not to understand, says Saint Catherine, that the Savior is requesting the removal of his Passion. In this ultimate prayer to his Father, Jesus is really asking for the removal of the cup that stands for the ill will of a human liberty that can turn the chalice of his life-giving blood into a cup of wrath giving eternal death.

According to Saint Catherine, this cup involved for Christ the need to patiently accept that his blood would not immediately bear all its fruit. He had to wait patiently and take upon himself all the delays, all the resistance that would be opposed to the accomplishment of grace. Saint Catherine insists a great deal on the fact that the Passion of Christ, his true passion, his divine passion, was the passion of desire and that his physical sufferings were nothing in comparison to the desire he had for the world's salvation, nothing compared to the suffering arising from the resistance he encountered in the contradictions of our hearts. Christ's temptation reaches its highest point of intensity through Judas, a friend whom Jesus had chosen as one of the twelve apostles but in the person of whom he now sees all those who trample in their hearts the fruit of his blood. This is what causes him to undergo agony and to sweat blood. As we have seen, blood flowed from Christ even before anyone struck him physically. The infinite love of God for his creatures, a love that is then ridiculed by them, awakens in the heart of Jesus an infinite amount of suffering. This sweating of blood surges in him from the depths of divine love, from the inside going to the outside. The opposite will be true during the actual Passion. The agony and the sweating of blood are really the epiphany of the wound inflicted on God's purely gratuitous love. In God himself, this wound can leave no trace, but it is given tangible expression in the human nature that God has assumed in the person of his Son. When Jesus says, "not my will, but yours," he agrees to be the instrument of the redemption in which his blood will have to go through the cup of our liberty. He accepts that the divine desire to save us, a desire of which he is the instrument and the expression, might remain forever unfulfilled in one or the other of God's children.

Here is revealed the mystery of the victorious acceptance by God of the radically unacceptable factor constituted by the contradiction of evil. What can the divine love do in the face of this contradiction if not love despite everything and against all odds? Thus on the night of Gethsemane, the covenant in the Lamb, sealed in his blood from the beginning of the world, was made manifest. God loves despite everything and against all odds, despite and against man's liberty; he will forever love man with the desire to make him blessed; he will love man despite everything, even despite man's self-imposed damnation.

Those Condemned to Hell, Pursued by Love

The mystical intuitions of Saint Catherine lead to an entire reflection on the mystery of damnation and hell. Under these conditions, if there are any people who have been condemned to hell, they remain nevertheless in God's heart, besieged on all sides by his love. They are somewhat like the black holes in the universe that absorb all luminous rays but without emitting or reflecting any light themselves. God is love. He cannot prevent himself from loving. He cannot cease from loving all the more those of his creatures who have driven themselves into such a contradictory state of being. If there are people condemned to hell, they will only be visible in

Christ's Mystical Body in a way comparable to the nail holes and side wound that remained in Jesus's glorified body after his resurrection. These people do not respond to love, but they are surrounded by love, forever pursued by the divine love that they have rejected by a definitive "no." Such is the veritable sin against the Holy Spirit, which consists not in a refusal to love but in the resolute decision not to be loved by God. It is the ultimate and total repugnance for God's love and for his kingdom, because these have become for the one who has damned himself a source not of happiness but of torment. The person damned to hell has become completely alienated, rebellious, and hostile with regard to love. Damnation is in fact the total revolt of liberty in someone who does not want to receive anything from God but who wants to exist entirely on his own. For such an individual, receiving love from another really does amount to "being in hell" in the literal sense of the term. Is there anyone among us who can claim never to have experienced, at one time or another in his life in this world, a small taste of what the possibility of hell and damnation represents? It is possible to taste not the actual reality of hell but the real possibility of going to hell for each and every one of us when out of pride we close ourselves to love and cease wanting to be loved because we do not want to accept the need of being loved in our poverty and in our nothingness. As Jesus said to Saint Catherine of Siena, "You are the one who is not, I am the one who is." If we do not accept our own nothingness, we cannot accept the love that drew us out of nothingness by creating us. "Make yourself capacity, that is, make yourself a space to be filled," continued Christ, speaking to Saint Catherine, "and I will be the stream of onrushing living water."

In this contemplation of Jesus's agony and his sweating of blood, it is amazing to see the way in which Love gives of itself despite the contradiction. "Not my will, but yours," said Jesus to the Father. That is to say, "I will love according to your plan, I will love this man until the end without considering the fact that this man could oppose and reject my love by definitively and eternally answering 'no.'" Such is the drama of hell: God cannot accommodate himself to our "no." Indeed if God could take into account and act on our "no," then it would be possible for him to do one of two things. On the one hand, he could suppress our being, as some claim he does, and then the damned would simply cease to exist. On the other hand, God could give us a form of happiness outside of himself.

This, however, is impossible, because God is Being. It is impossible to remain in existence outside of him, and because he is also and at the same time Love, it is impossible not be loved by him. So what can God do other than continue in his love for us, blindfolded against a refusal of love that remains inconceivable to him? God insists on loving us in hand-to-hand combat with our liberties, right down to our last breath.

And even beyond our last breath, if ever our liberty were to become anchored in a final refusal, he would continue to love us anyway, even though it would seem to be a pure loss. But it is precisely this folly of mercy that accomplishes immanently, in a paradoxical manner, the requirements of justice. Even Satan is a being pursued by God's love. This is clearly illustrated in the book of Job, where Satan appears before God with the other angels and converses with the Lord. He is later cast out of heaven because although he came to accuse man, his accusations were discredited. Henceforth he is no longer able to tempt God. But despite this, he is not banished outside of God's love. That would be impossible, for God cannot establish a creature outside of being. The so-called outer darkness in which Satan now dwells is a space that exists only in the context of a created being's liberty, a liberty that has freely chosen to reject God's love. To be in the outer darkness does not really mean to dwell away from the presence of God. On the contrary, the same presence of God, which for the saints is the source of happiness and joy, is the torment of Satan because of his pride and jealousy. The cup of blessing has become for him the cup of wrath.

The Self-Punishment of Hell

It is clear that the righteousness of God is inseparable from his love. It is therefore diametrically opposed to a revengeful type of justice. Hell is indeed a punishment, but as such it derives from an immanent form of justice, in which the damned punish themselves. God continues to give that which he promised. Justice for him consists in not going back on his word: he promised the gift of being, and he gives it. He cannot cease to maintain in existence one of his spiritual creatures. He promised eternal life in his presence, and this is what he gives. The person who is made miserable by this gift can only blame himself for voluntarily transforming happiness into misfortune.

We ourselves are our own tormentors. If at the time of the last judgment one of the damned were capable of saying, "Lord, miserable creature that I am, what have I done with my life?" the love of God would immediately encompass him. If there could be found in one of the damned anything similar to the repentant sorrow that is sometimes seen in death row inmates who mourn their fate when their death sentence is pronounced, if there was something like that in any person damned to hell, it would open all the floodgates of God's mercy in his heart. But damnation implies that a person has hardened his heart in a last stand against mercy, so that mercy itself becomes for him an endless source of suffering. The slightest movement, if not of love, at least of the need to be loved, would cause God to react as did the father in the gospel parable when the prodigal son returned home. In the parable, the father even overlooks the fact that the son's motivations are still selfish. Indeed, the prodigal son did not come home motivated at first by repentance. He returned pushed by dire need, saying to himself, "In my father's house, even the servants eat better than I eat now." It was not a glorious motivation, but it was sufficient because he agreed to be loved by the Father, as did the good thief on the cross. No one is condemned to hell simply because of a refusal to love; if the opposite were true, who could avoid damnation? We will only be damned if we refuse to be loved. Unfortunately we can learn progressively, on a day-to-day basis, to make this refusal through pride, which causes us to forget or "unlearn" how to love. And as we become more and more incapable of loving, we end up by despairing of God's love. Those who refuse to love no longer know what it is to love, and they soon begin to think that love amounts to a pure deception. And then, little by little, they find it unbearable to be loved in this world, or to see people around them who love one another. We know that something of this tendency resides in each one of our hearts, like a latent germ or virus that carries contagion from hell. The disease itself becomes clearly visible in some people who seem already to be leading a hellish existence here on earth. We need only think of certain families, of certain couples in which hatred has taken root. Is it not true that the reality of hell is foreshadowed in situations where love has become unbearable?

In the Crucible of Eternal Love

Need we despair? No, on the contrary. Saint Catherine of Siena invites us to enter into the night of Gethsemane, not in order to allow ourselves to be overwhelmed, but so that we can find strength there. A sentence of Christ sums it all up: "Am I not to drink of the cup that the Father has given me?" (John 18:11).

The cup of man's delirium has been taken up by God into the hand of his love. God will love us "unto the very end," that is, until the last breath of our liberty; and no matter what happens, he will pursue us with his love for all eternity. Our liberty is in his hand, in the hand of his love. God can only be Love in regard to our liberty, and therefore everything is possible; hope remains until the last breath of our earthly existence. All Saint Catherine's apostolic intercessory prayers have their source in this cell of the mercy of God's heart. It is here that Saint Catherine brings together, in a unique contemplation of Love in its source, all the tearful pleadings of her intercession and all the words proclaimed in her apostolic mission. Everything comes together in this cell, everything is played out here, because until the end of the world, it is the scene of hand-to-hand combat between God and our liberty, a liberty that does not exist outside of or apart from the Lord but is situated in the most intimate cell of his fatherly heart. This cell is the mystery of the Lamb. It is a mystery collected in the cup of our liberty, a mystery that envelops our freedom, which it tightly embraces, just as the angel in Genesis held Jacob tightly in his grip as the two of them fought together. As the great contemplative witness to the mystery of the Lamb, Saint Catherine was powerfully inspired to intercede and to preach without ever leaving the cell of the heart of God where the drama of human freedom or liberty takes place.

The mystery of the Lamb is the direct opposite of a scenario written in advance: we can pray for the salvation of all men, including Judas. In God's design there is neither past nor future. There is only the eternity of God who accompanies by his grace in present time the liberty of men, who are held together in the fellowship of his love.

The mystery of the Lamb does not give rise to a spirituality of "consolation," in the way that this has sometimes been expressed in certain insufficiently profound devotions to the heart of Jesus. Christ does not ask us to kneel beside him at Gethsemane so that we can say, "Behold, O Lord, although others do not love you, I will accompany you; please be consoled in my heart, let my heart be the stone upon which you can rest your head." But here we have exactly the opposite. Along with Saint Catherine of Siena, we enter the cell of Gethsemane in order to boldly ask God for everything, for the salvation of all sinners; we dare to enter into direct combat with the most apparently insurmountable refusals, with the most desperate situations. The cell of the Lamb's mercy in the heart of the Father also belongs to Jesus, who said, "Knock, and it will be opened to you."

Saint Catherine was so profoundly permeated by this experience that at a key moment, when she was confronted with the refusal of a soul, she boldly said to God, "I demand." I demand the salvation of that soul. This would be folly if we did not see that in the cell of mercy this "I demand" is the equivalent of "your will be done." Such a prayer really does correspond to the will of God, but God is awaiting "cups" who will receive and contain this will. "I will not go forth from your presence," said Saint Catherine one day, "until I see that you have had mercy on your people. And what good would it do me to see that I have life, if your people remain in death, if darkness envelops your Bride, the Church. Have pity on your people! Have mercy on everyone, I beseech you, in virtue of the uncreated Love that inspired you to create man in your image and according to your likeness."

We have here the central phrase concerning the mystery of the Lamb: the uncreated love in the heart of God the Father. God created man in his image and likeness, establishing with him a covenant that even the most radical contradiction of sin cannot destroy: "He first loved us" (1 John 4:19).

"O God, My Mercy!"

Saint Catherine gives us the key to the well-known night prayer of Saint Dominic, the only prayer of his that has been transmitted. When Saint Dominic prayed, his brothers were astonished to hear him "howling and wailing from the depths of his heart" as he repeated, "O My Mercy" — he called God "my mercy" — "what will become of sinners?" Saint Dominic dwells in the cell of mercy, in the presence of the mystery of the cup.

And whenever he feels that he is about to capitulate before the contradiction of sin, in the face of the resistance and the damnation of sinners, he precipitates himself into the arms of God, shouting, "O My Mercy." In him, in the Lamb, Saint Dominic finds the strength to hope against all odds, to love against all odds; he adopts the Lamb as his personal seal.

To enter into the cell of mercy is to enter into God's desire. The cry of Jesus on the cross, "I thirst," strongly impressed Saint Catherine. It was the thirst for man's faith, a thirst he already expressed to the Samaritan woman, the thirst to have men receive his love. Jesus told Saint Catherine that his suffering on the cross was like nothing compared to the torment of his desire. "It was love," says Saint Catherine, "that attached Jesus Christ to the Cross, not the nails. His cross was a cross of desire."

One enters into the cell of mercy in virtue of the nothingness of the creature. The nothingness of the creature is like a cup, like a hollow space in which being is poured by creative love. "You are made only of love," said Saint Catherine. This formula helps explain the ultimate meaning of her other well-known statement, "My nature is fire." Everything here is coherent: perceiving that we are those who are not, that by ourselves we are nothing, we must avoid the harmful intoxication of the cup by making ourselves pure "capacity" in which it is possible to receive the torrent of the love of God the Father.

We must implore the mercy of the heart of the Father in the name of the nothingness from which he has derived his creatures; this nothingness serves like a whiff of fresh air, which draws into itself the flame of God's love. It is not in the name of our good works or in virtue of any merit whatsoever that we can invoke mercy. We can do to so only in the name of God: "For the glory of your name, do not repudiate your covenant."

That which apparently separates us most from God, the fact that he is Being and that we are nothingness, the fact that he is the Holy One and we are sinners, is the very thing that urges us to run and offer ourselves entirely to him. It is useless for us to search for a few good works that we could present on our own behalf to the Lord, since we might only hear him respond through the prophet Isaiah, "all our righteous deeds are like a filthy cloth" (Isa. 64:6). Instead, as sinners, we must precipitate ourselves into God's arms, exposing in his presence our nothingness. It is when we are truly able to say to God, "I am the one who is not," that he can respond, "It is I who make you exist." It is when we say to God, "I have sinned," that he says to us, "I give you my forgiveness and I love you." When we place ourselves in the most radical truth of our condition, we can obtain everything, not only for ourselves, but also for others.

The cell of mercy is the heart of God the Father that carries the mystery of the Lamb. Saint Dominic and Saint Catherine, who were apostles during the day, never really left the inner cells in which they always enclosed themselves during the solitude of their nights. After the service of compline, Saint Dominic remained in prayer, and Saint Catherine did so too in her cell, until the hour when she heard the bell for matins ringing in the nearby convent of the brothers. This extremely solitary prayer in the secret cell of the Father's mercy has at the same time a missionary character, because it espouses from within God's desire for our salvation, as well as the hand-to-hand combat of the Lord's eternal love with our liberty that always operates in the present moment and that is encompassed in the mystery of the Lamb.

> No one will snatch them [my sheep] out of my hand.
> What my Father has given me is greater than all else,
> and no one can snatch it out of the Father's hand.
> (John 10:28–29)

PART THREE

An Understanding of the Mystery

Let us learn to despise the absurd
and worship the mystery

*The mysterious and hidden wisdom of God . . .
that which no human mind has conceived.*

—1 Corinthians 2:7, 9

CHAPTER ELEVEN

God without the Idea of Evil

It may seem presumptuous to proclaim in today's world that God does not have the idea of evil and, even more radically, that he has no idea whatsoever of evil. Does this not amount to a provocation or to imagining God as some sort of "angelic" abstraction removed from a part of reality?

Nevertheless, I chose for my book the title *God without the Idea of Evil* because the expression itself, which comes from Saint Thomas Aquinas, ended up by astonishing and dazzling me. Saint Thomas is a great doctor of the church who does not generally allow himself to be carried away by words and who always speaks in a very precise and theologically formal manner. Like many other theology students, I first came across this phrase long ago, in the *Summa Theologiae*, but without at the time fully grasping its meaning or its many implications. I was able to discover all this only later, thanks to a great twentieth-century theologian, Jacques Maritain, together with his wife, Raïssa. This couple gave an impressive witness to the innocence of God amid an existence in which suffering was far from absent and in a world shaken by the worst manifestations of ideological hatred, racism, and totalitarianism, terrible plagues of hell that were let loose during the twentieth century. It so happens that this man and this woman were converts. Having been dazzled by the innocence of God, they were able to help those around them to discover it too by their life consecrated to theological research and especially through the spiritual experience on which that research was based.

In the old days, it was quite common to refer to God as the "Good Lord." I would make bold to say in an absolute manner that *God is good*. I would make this affirmation humbly, following in the footsteps of the two great above-mentioned witnesses of the twentieth century and echoing the words of Saint Thomas Aquinas: "God has no idea of evil."

When confronting the scandal of evil, two solutions come to mind. The first is to deny God because of evil. We have all heard others saying and we perhaps surprise ourselves by thinking, "If God really existed, the world would not be as it is." But to deny God because of the scandal of evil is perhaps not, in the final analysis, the worst solution. Let us listen to Raïssa Maritain. In her diary she writes, "To deny God because *all of nature is groaning* [as if in the pangs of childbirth; see Rom. 8:22] is only an effort to relieve God of responsibility for having made creation in such a way that suffering is inevitable. This is proof that we have such a natural love of God (inscribed in nature itself) that, even when it remains hidden in the depths of the subconscious, we still have the desire to absolve God of all the evil suffered by men."[1] To deny God because of evil is to at least understand that God cannot be bound up with evil. Does this not amount, in an obscure way, to speaking after the manner of Job? In this area it is perhaps better to speak like Job, or even to resort to an excessive negation of God, rather than remain in the blasphemy of Job's friends, who in their theodicy claimed to explain how God includes evil in his design.

The other alternative, which corresponds to the royal road of the Christian faith, is to positively discover that the innocent God really exists and that it is he who is the living and one true God. Paradoxically, I quote as a witness to God's innocence the nineteenth-century poet Lautréamont, of whom it has been said that he carried, in his revolt against the abominations of this world, the "good news of damnation." "If we remember," he said, "that the absolute goodness of God and his absolute ignorance of evil is the truth from which all the other truths derive, then all sophistic fallacies will collapse by themselves."[2] This phrase seeks deliberately to create a shocking effect. Lautréamont speaks exorbitantly, not only of a God who has no idea of evil, but of a God who is absolutely ignorant of evil. Here, without a doubt, he is going too far. The gospel of Saint John says of Jesus, "[He] needed no one to testify about anyone; for he himself knew what was in everyone" (2:25). And the Bible often tells us that God probes all minds and hearts.

No, if God does not conceive evil, this is not due to the fact that something escapes his knowledge. Lautréamont, however, rightly sensed that God is in no way the inventor of evil, not even as an author who writes evil into his script. Jacques Maritain fought hard to uproot from the conscience of Christians this idea of a God who has written in advance a drama in which evil has already been programmed, of a God who has opted for introducing evil into his design as an element that is of course purely negative but nevertheless useful. Often we do not think of God, writes Maritain,

> as a Father whose will is flouted, treated with contempt, at every moment by his children, in the incoercible liberty which is their amazing privilege (hence creating the need for divine super-compensations), but instead, as an emperor after the manner of this world, a potentate-playwright who is himself the first author of the sins of the world and of all its misery, through the permissions which he grants to fail, permissions which *precede* our actual failures, and where in advance he abandons the creature to itself. And we then go on to imagine that he is actually pleased with this spectacle of human history which he himself has arranged and where evil abounds in an abominable way. It is this absurd and intolerable idea that lies at the bottom of the revolt against God of a vast number of non-Christians, the idea of a potentate-playwright who remains insensitive, in his heaven, to the evil endured by the characters whom he causes to perform his play.[3]

Those who rebel against this idea of God as a "potentate-playwright" seem to provide us, as did Job in the Old Testament, with a hollow mold or photographic negative of the true God, proving that our conscience cannot resign itself to any such blasphemy. And yet the idea of a God who has written a script that includes evil still continues to gnaw away at our Christian subconscious.

But if God has no idea of evil, it is that there is not in him any intelligible matrix of evil. God cannot conceive evil, because all that God conceives he creates as being, goodness, life. The "ideas" of God are the ways in which his creatures participate in his perfections. As for evil, it *is not*, and therefore God cannot know it through an idea. There is nothing in him that corresponds to evil.

Evil, I have said, *is not*. But this affirmation is insufficient. Many people feel revolted when they are told that evil is not, and rightly so, since we can all see the havoc caused by evil in the lives of men. We cannot stop there. Evil is not a "something"; but neither is it the simple negation of "something." It is not only an absence; it is a deprivation. Its deficiency resides in the fact that it is a disorder constituted by a disordered relationship between two goods. Manichaean dualism, which threatens us continually in this domain, would have us imagine evil as a malicious power having some kind of existence in itself. This is not the case. A few examples may help us understand. We say that an earthquake is an "evil"; but an earthquake is the working of a force of nature, powerful and beautiful in itself, just as a volcanic eruption can be. An earthquake is an evil when it relates to and harms in its integrity a reality far greater and higher than the cosmic forces, namely, the human person, called by grace to immortality. When things like earthquakes or microbes infringe on a higher good, this disorder provokes in us a feeling of "revolt."

It is important to distinguish between evil in the proper or absolute sense of the term and the evils that constitute the portion of disorder inherent in creation and are only evils of "imperfection." (This inherent imperfection is indicated by the book of Genesis: The world, when it was first created, is said to have been "without form, and void" ("tohu" and "bohu") (Gen. 1:2 KJV). The real, absolute evil is that which affects the human person. Even animal pain does not affect a being called by grace to immortality, and therefore it cannot be identified purely and simply with the suffering and death endured by human beings. Evil is scandalous when it affects a person. This indicates that its source must be sought in the person himself. If by his own initiative with regard to nothingness, by his own sin, man had not fallen below the state of cosmic royalty that was his and that is alluded to in scripture (Gen. 1:26), he would not have had to submit passively to the cosmic cycle of generation and corruption but would on the contrary have dominated it. He would have referred it to a new and definitive order, the order of justice and charity, which carries the fruit of immortality.

But why then did God make man fallible? Let us listen once again to Jacques Maritain.

> The peccability of the creature is . . . a ransom for the outpouring of the creative Goodness of God, who, in order to *give himself personally* to the point of transforming into himself someone other than himself, must be *loved freely in a love of friendship*. And in order to be loved freely in a love of friendship, he had to make creatures who are *free*, and in order to make them free, he had to make them *fallible* in their liberty. Without fallible liberty, there is no created liberty; without created liberty, there can be no love of friendship between God and the creature; without a love of friendship between God and the creature, there can be no supernatural transformation of the creature into God, no entry of the created person into the joy of his Lord.[4]

Ultimately, one cannot blame the Creator for having loved us too much. Here we must dare to repeat the beautiful expression of the Eastern fathers who speak of the "folly" of God's love for men.

Because he invited us to make the preferential choice required by the love of friendship, because he wanted us to choose him for what he is in himself, God put us on the path of a turbulent creation. But he also came to walk with us, like someone who begs and supplicates, asking us to love him above all else. We are on a journey across a cosmos whose order is incomplete; and our ultimate Good, the Beloved, gives himself to us as in the guise of Christ the pilgrim, as he was depicted in the Middle Ages. We must discover him hidden under the species of the particular goods among which he teaches us to establish an order by fastening the desire of our hearts to him alone. From threshold to threshold, from one beginning to the next, we learn to prefer God's love, which will ultimately be revealed as the great secret of the Trinitarian life into which the Lord wants to introduce us.

By creating people in the world, God introduced aspirations that go beyond the world.

> It is only . . . when a free and intelligent creature loves God *by virtue of its freedom* . . . with a love chosen as a free option, that it loves Him above all else as an object of a love which goes to Him independently of any created object, a love which goes only to God insomuch as He it is separated from everything else in His absolute singularity. (It is a direct love of God, an act set apart, without intermediary, going from person to person). The reason for this is that the act of free will as such is not *of this world*; in the natural order itself, it does not belong to the world of creation, to the world of that which has been made—that is why the angels, who are entitled to know all that belongs to the world of creation, do not know the secrets of the heart. . . . [T]he person, going beyond this world, crosses without any intermediary the chasm between the created and the uncreated, in order to give itself to the Uncreated.[5]

If God had not created us as persons in his image and likeness (Gen. 1:27), the world would have been sufficient for us. We would have been happy there if we had been created so as to be proportionate to it. But we can only be miserable even in a better world, in the "best of all possible worlds" imagined by philosophers, since we were made for something other than the world. In a hypothetical "best of all worlds," we would probably be even more inconsolable at not having God. The world is for us the location of a slow deciphering of the face of someone who is beyond this world: the face of the Creator. "Our heart is restless," wrote Saint Augustine at the beginning of the *Confessions*, "until it rests in you." The "best of all possible worlds" would be nothing more than an "air-conditioned nightmare." We would be satisfied on the natural level, yet we would lack everything. Blessed is that which is missing in this chaotic creation through which God the pilgrim passes, the God who visited Abraham in his nomad's tent at the Oak of Mamre.

Since the original sin, we have ignored God's love that would have made us kings of creation; and we have therefore been subjected to the experience of suffering that comes from the cosmic disorder that now imprisons us, even when we think that we have dominated it by our technical progress. It would suffice to recall the costly adverse effects of the imbalances entailed by the exploitation of natural resources, or simply the degradation of the life-sustaining environment, all of which are inevitable consequences of technological progress, which in itself is a good thing. Cardinal Charles Journet, a disciple and friend of Maritain, sees the human condition as twofold.

> As *individuals*, human persons are part of the cosmic order; but as *persons*, each one constitutes a unity in itself which belongs to the trans-cosmic world of liberty. In the first case (that of the individual), evil appears as simply the *reverse, negative aspect of the cosmic order*. . . . In the second case (on the personal level), the same evil takes on the additional aspect of antagonizing and frustrating the "trans-natural" aspirations of the person. . . . [T]hese desires are conditional, and they can be forever frustrated, but grace can fill them. . . . The state of original integrity and the transforming gifts of original grace are so much in line with the desires of our human nature, that we cannot help but think that God, although he could have, in his infinite liberty, denied them to us, nevertheless had to grant them, since their absence in us would seem to result from some initial misfortune which has also taken on the character of an injury or a penalty. . . . Does not a mother who cries over the death of her child,—as Rachel, who did "not want to be comforted" is said to have done (Jer. 31:15 and Matt. 2:18)—perhaps have an obscure inkling of what man's condition was in the beginning? Could not her cry perhaps be a recourse to the first design of creative goodness, an impossible desire of paradise lost? For indeed, God, in his loving tenderness, had prepared another life, and it was under the rays of a transfiguring grace that our journey in time ought to have been accomplished.[6]

Sin frustrates above all the transcosmic aspirations of the human person, and nothing in this world can either explain or console the untold sufferings that have been caused as a result. Against all the "theodicies" advanced by Job's friends, in the past or in the present, Jacques Maritain writes, "Sin, as a disaster for this whole which is the person, and as an offense against God, together with the suffering and pain that follow as consequences of sin, all this was not permitted for the greater perfection of the machine of the universe, but for the consumption of a labor of love that transcends the entire order of the world; all this must be referred to . . . the transfiguration through love . . . of created persons who have become *God by participation*."[7] The sufferings of the human person are incomparable to the neurological pain of the animal, even if they seem to be identical; and similarly the human sufferings of the divine person of the incarnate Word in the "form of a slave" (Phil. 2:7) are incommensurate with the same sufferings in a created person. The extent of suffering is commensurate with the dignity of the person whom it affects.

But if the human person as the primary cause of moral evil is solely responsible for its own disaster, how does God know evil in its free origin, he who has no idea of evil? The time has come to speak of God's delicately discreet modesty.

God does not conceive evil, first of all because he does not anticipate or foresee the liberty that can cause it. We have here the delicately discreet modesty of the eternal Lord. The Eternal One always accompanies our liberties in the present moment. Very lucky indeed are those who know that God is the Eternal One, that he is a gushing fountain of youth that renews us at every moment. As we see in the episode of the good thief on the cross, every act of our liberty is an absolute beginning in God's grace, because God is the Eternal One, and he gives his grace in present time to our liberty. God does not anticipate or foresee our actions, because for him, says Saint Thomas Aquinas, "nothing is in the future." Jacques Maritain has left liberating lines on this subject: "The good of the creature endowed with liberty, can only be known in the very moment when it is desired . . . because generally, the constellation of all the various created causes is unable to make known in advance with certainty, the act of a free will, which as such, depends only on itself and on the first cause."[8]

In other words, although God knows all our good acts, of which he is the first source, he does not know them by anticipation or prediction, because freedom itself is unpredictable. Cardinal Charles Journet explains this brilliantly:

> God alone sees future events[,] . . . not as more or less predetermined in their causes (in this sense, divine science is not a *prescience or foreknowledge*); but directly in themselves, by an eternal knowledge that is immutable, fathoming the depths, capturing each event in the freshness of its coming into existence (in that sense this divine science is

really a super-science. . . . The ancient sophistic fallacies that have opposed God's foreknowledge and human freedom, derive from attempts to pull God down from eternity into time, after which, once He has been stripped of his super-science, the only thing left to do is to attribute to Him by anthropomorphism our human concept of foreknowledge which pertains only to that which is predetermined.[9]

God does not make predictions about our liberty in the way that a meteorologist forecasts the weather. God does not engage in speculations about our future actions. The Lord does not need to have recourse to any so-called super-comprehension of causes to foresee our free acts, since he actually knows them from the inside and in the present moment by giving us the ability to accomplish them. At the moment when we have completed making our confession, God does not speculate on or count in advance our future failures. Since God has the delicate discreet modesty of the Eternal One, we ought to respect this modesty for ourselves and for others.

The eternal Lord is not in time: nothing is for him either in the past or in the future; everything is in the present in his actual "effectuation." This is something impossible for us to represent; it is useless to try to make imaginative efforts. Each one of us simply needs to say to ourselves the following: God sees me only in my "today," and as for my tomorrow, he knows it such as that tomorrow becomes my today, but never in the way that it still is for me a tomorrow. This is the greatest truth of the biblical revelation concerning the living God, inseparable from the truth affirming that there is only one God. It is not by simple chance that in the Bible God is named the "Eternal."

God is not a spectator of our human liberty that he inhabits and animates by his grace. He is not that cold eye observing us from within the triangle, according to an obscene representation of God produced by rationalism, which has invaded Christian art. It is a shameless caricature of the God of the Bible, the God who before the woman who had been caught committing adultery obstinately kept his eyes lowered, for as long as her accusers, egged on by Satan the Accuser, persisted in trying to make him take note of her sin.

It is true that God implicitly knows the physical imperfection of the universe that he creates, because he wants it indirectly as the inevitable reverse side of the world that he has chosen as the road for the growth of our liberty. But as for moral evil, God does not know it in a preliminary decision to allow it. Strictly speaking, God does not allow evil. He allows the liberty that can cause it; but, let me repeat it once again, the possibility of sin inherent in created liberty, considering that man is created in grace, is in no way a necessity, unlike physical evil, which is the necessary reverse side of an unfinished cosmic order. God from the beginning of Genesis comes to hold the hand of his child in the first steps of its liberty. Eucharistic Prayer IV addresses the Father, saying, "When man had lost your friendship, turning away from you, you did not give him into the power of death. In your mercy, you came to the aid of all men so that they could seek you and find you." How could we think that by a withdrawal of his grace and by a permission to fail made prior to our sins, God would already, in one way or another, have known these sins in advance and would have "made allowances" for them, which comes down to saying that he would already in advance have resigned himself to sending people to hell?

God does not conceive, even indirectly, sin, moral evil in its source. God knows moral evil in all the consequences that result from sinful choices: the degradation of our souls and bodies, the deterioration of our family and social ties. But the root of sin is a lack of attention to the love that is God, a nonconsideration of the Lord himself as a standard of absolute good, a nonadherence to the motion of his grace. This fissure of nothingness in our liberty, which commands the evil act, has not yet caused any deprivations in us before we commit any sinful act. Its "nothingness" is a complete frustration of the prevenient grace that seeks to foster our growth in the good; by this nothingness we count purely for nothing the divine love as the source of grace. Following Origen, the Greek fathers such as Saint Gregory of Nyssa and Saint Maximus the Confessor questioned themselves concerning this mysterious "satiety" of a liberty that "having had its fill of" the grace given by God ceases in its self-sufficiency to consider the Lord himself as the absolute Good and as the norm or standard for making choices.

The nonconsideration of grace, which is the cause of all sin, does not in itself deprive our liberty of anything. God knows it only as a pure insult to his free love. The nonconsideration of grace flouts God's love by willfully ignoring it but without yet contradicting it by the sinful choices that will bring on disaster. God receives this lack of attention to his love, by which we remove ourselves freely from the working of his grace, as a blow to his heart. Such an attack is impossible to ward off, it is incomprehensible, unknowable other than as a pure frustration of the gratuitous love of God for us, as the indefinable "suffering of God," which, in the creature, is not yet a deficiency and, in the Creator, is already an affront to his subsisting love that knows no lack. Jacques Maritain describes it admirably: sin is an offense against God, an injury inflicted on God, not on his being, but on his gratuitous love for his creatures.

> Sin destroys something in the order of creation, it does not destroy anything in God. . . . [It] deprives the divine will of something it really wanted. . . . In his antecedent will, God wants all men to be saved, he also wants all my acts to be good. If I sin, something that God wanted and loved will not be eternally. And that happens through my primary initiative. . . . Here, we can say that God is the most vulnerable of beings. No need for poisoned arrows, cannons or machine guns, just an invisible movement in the heart of a free agent is enough to injure and deprive His antecedent will of something here below that He wanted and loved from all eternity.[10]

The first cause of the evil coming from our liberty is "known" by God in a mysterious acceptance at seeing his love for us frustrated and ridiculed. This is like the "dead center" of our will by which man already shrinks away from the influx of grace, even before committing a deliberate act of refusal. When it no longer considers grace the measuring standard of the absolute Good, our liberty can no longer make an act of choice without sinning. This "dead center" is the first fissure of nothingness in the act of our liberty. It is as obscure as "the hour of darkness" into which Jesus sinks at Gethsemane. It is for God the great unacceptable thing of which he has no idea and which he can only endure by seizing it in a victorious acceptance of salvation in Jesus Christ. "The image of the crucified Jesus," says Raïssa Maritain, "is like an expression of pain in God, an expression of what pain could be in the divine essence,"[11] and again: "The virtual suffering exceeds the present suffering (*the suffering of Jesus in heaven*); and it is found in love."[12] These mystical intuitions were admirably commented on by Jacques Maritain at the end of his life: "The eternal splendor of the victorious Acceptance . . . we have no proper way of naming . . . [has made itself known to us] in the image par excellence, the image of flesh and blood of the Son of God suffering death."[13] God sets his eyes on evil only at the very movement when, as in the episode of the adulterous woman, his love seizes it in order to give salvation and forgiveness.

If it is possible for us to elude the divine motion, this is because the growth in the good that grace produces in us is an object of faith that, as such, requires our free acquiescence. God's grace destined for our beatitude, because it has to deify us, must deliver us from our limits as creatures. Even without sin, as in the case of the Virgin Mary, or as it would have been in the case of Eve and Adam had they not fallen, grace necessarily involves a deification that goes through a "Passover." One does not pass from the created state to the uncreated without paying a price: "It is a fearful thing to fall into the hands of the living God" (Heb. 10:31). One does not enter into the consuming fire of the Trinitarian life without going through a death to oneself in view of a resurrection for God.

Raïssa Maritain has transmitted to us on this topic the fruit of her own spiritual experience.

> Sacrifice is an absolutely general law for the creature on its road to perfection. Anything that passes from a lower to a higher nature, must go through self-sacrifice, mortification and death.[14]

> That which must be removed from human love,—to render it pure, benevolent, universal, and divine—is not the love itself; no, that which must be removed or rather surpassed, are the limits of the heart. That is where the suffering comes from—in this effort to grow out of our narrow limits. For it is in those limits, in our limits, that our human joy lies. . . . This really involves dying to ourselves.[15]

> This law of the transformation of natures—which embraces in itself all moral and divine laws—is something necessary, something as it were physical, ontological—God himself cannot abolish it, since he cannot produce anything that is absurd. But this law—the Law—is not He himself—He is Love. . . . And as for us, He has revealed to us

all the fearful demands for the deification of man.... When nature, confronted with the need to obey, groans and suffers, it is not rendered despicable in God's eyes, for indeed, leaving one's own form is for any nature a loss—and for the sensitive nature it involves suffering.... [The law] is opposed in a certain manner, to love. It is as the Creator that God made the law. But because He is also the final end and our Beatitude, He calls us to go beyond.... It (the law) is really a necessity; but it is *only* a necessity. Love gives us something over and above the Law. [It forgives.][16]

When we perceive that grace will inevitably make us go through a painful Passover of nature, then, at some point, we put our will into "neutral," we cease to adhere to the influence of a God who inexorably wants us to be holy as he is holy. And our liberty thus slips from between God's hands, because we have ceased to have faith in his loving countenance, we have failed to recognize that face filled with love that lies behind the requirement to grow in the Good, a growth that necessarily strips us of ourselves. And thus the first act that we accomplish when we lack faith no longer refers to the Other par excellence who is God: this act will be a sin, a disorder in regard to the good that comes from him. Jesus wept over Jerusalem, "If you, even you, had only recognized on this day the things that make for peace! But now they are hidden from your eyes . . . because you did not recognize the time of your visitation" (Luke 19:42–44). The publicans Zaccheus and Matthew, as well as many other sinners, have been saved simply by allowing Jesus to visit them. "I am standing at the door, knocking" (Rev. 3:20).

But if we "make nothing of, or consider as worthless," the gratuitous love of God who visits us in his grace, do you think that God turns away from us? Spiritual authors often say things like, "I fear Jesus who passes by and then does not return." The Council of Trent itself says that "God only abandons those who have first abandoned him." But the goal of these fear-inspiring words is to warn us against the progressive hardening of the heart of our liberty that can ultimately lead us to our final damnation. When Jesus on the cross proclaims, "My God, my God, why have you forsaken me?" it is not the hard-heartedness of the Father that he is expressing but rather the hardness of the heart of men when they definitively turn their backs on God. In Jesus, God has "loved [us] to the end" (John 13:1). If we slam the door in the face of God's love, he does not turn and go away; his prevenient grace, as Saint Thomas says, immediately sets out to "harass us," to win us over. The hard-heartedness of our liberty is like a fortress besieged by divine love, and if God cannot enter through the door, he tries to enter through the windows, or even through the basement. On the cross, and especially at Gethsemane, the Son of God showed us how God was taking hold of our most extreme refusals so that there would be no type of hard-heartedness that was not be visited by his grace. "God proves his love for us in that while we were sinners Christ died for us" (Rom. 5:8).

At the hour of death, grace tends to produce in the hearts of men works that are nothing short of miraculous. At that moment, grace produces free acceptances where liberty barely needs to make an act of choice. This does not mean that there is no longer any liberty. But liberty perhaps does not reside essentially in a choice between good and evil but in surrendering to grace and in the giving of one's consent to the ultimate good. When God visits his children in the hand-to-hand combat of the last struggle of agony or in the interval between clinical death and real death, in an instant that he alone knows and that undoubtedly contains the secret of Gethsemane and of Christ's descent into hell (1 Pet. 3:19–20), he places liberty at the edge of an indescribable bliss.

I would not dare say any of this if I could not quote here the words of Cardinal Journet, words that are so full of hope:

> I think that miraculous conversions . . . are very numerous, and that, because of the merits and prayers of the saints and friends of God, many big sinners are converted at the very last moment of their life. . . . [P]eople who may have lived far away from God, will, at the last moment, go over to God without anyone being aware of it. Perhaps they will even have appeared to have refused the gift of grace. I have in mind a short story of Lucian Marsaux. A girl lives with her father who no longer believes; she prays constantly for his conversion. And then the moment of death comes. She boldly puts the question to him: can I go to look for a priest? At these words, the soul of the father is illuminated: this is what he secretly desired; he wants to say yes, but his ges-

tures betray him, he makes a sign which means no, and he dies. Sometimes the external gesture betrays the will of the soul. . . . [T]here may be a dislocation between the soul and its envelope.[17]

It is therefore only by a hardening of the heart against love itself, the "sin against the Holy Spirit" (a sin that is almost no longer "human" since it adheres so closely to the angelic sin of Satan), that man at the last moment of liberty can choose for himself eternal damnation. Because it is God who saves by his grace, it can suffice for obtaining salvation to consent to the Lord's love at the final instant: "And love can save man even at the last moment of a bad life—if at that moment the man finds the light of love—perhaps if he believed that God is love."[18] On the other hand, because it is man who damns himself in opting against grace, such a decision requires a positive choice of evil as such. "In the final analysis," writes Jacques Maritain, "to be punished is simply to have that which one wanted. It means having the fruit wrapped in the act. When it is a question of the supreme and decisive act of our will, then we can say that the person really does want the fruit as well as the act. The saint prefers God and eternal life; but he who is damned prefers hell."[19]

What type of knowledge does God have of the supreme refusal of his grace, that of damnation? Since God only knows the refusals constituted by our sins in the gift itself of his prevenient grace, God knows the ultimate refusal of the damned, that of Satan, in the patience of a mysterious love that (in regard to them) is eternally held in check. As I said earlier, we must not imagine that the damned are far from the heart of God: they are surrounded by his love, which for their obdurate liberty becomes the fire of hell. God only knows their refusal in the desolate stupefaction of his love that has been flouted. Again Journet shows that the "outer darkness" is really only the inner darkness of an obdurate liberty that is completely refractory to the love that is God: "By refusing his love [the damned] triumph over God but by ransacking themselves. God, on his part, cannot stop loving them. . . . *The gift of God who created them out of love is without repentance.* If by an impossible hypothesis, God were to stop loving them, their revolt would suddenly become pointless, their sin would cease, hell would immediately disappear. If God could stop for a moment being the Love that wants to create and to deify, hell would vanish immediately."[20]

As for Maritain, he invites us to purify from any anthropomorphic idea of revenge the biblical notion of the "wrath of God": "Eternal justice must be designated, if we want to seek human images, less as a mysterious anger than as the mysterious patience of God, who endures having his mercy ultimately denied, and seeing one of his creatures become its own god, forever and of its own free choice. In this sense, which is infinitely more profound than in the case of punishments meted out during life here on earth, man gets what he wanted."[21]

God has no idea of evil. It is only in the hand-to-hand combat with our fallible liberty, in the present moment of our acts, that God "knows" evil by taking it up into his redeeming love. "It is quite true," writes Maritain,

> that in this way of looking at things, the Creator of the world does not treat himself to the restful spectacle of marionettes acting out a program that he himself designed for evil as well as for good. It is true that in this manner of looking at things, God wants us to engage wholeheartedly in the battle, because he himself in the first place has committed to it the glory of his name, or let me rather say, he has committed himself entirely, by sending his Son, one in nature with him. . . . [T]he work of God involves risks, real risks, because the drama is not only simply acted out, it is actually lived.[22]

In this design of grace, the economy that God organizes in the present time of the acts of our liberty, the game is not determined in advance. "The divine plan," says Cardinal Journet, "is not a scenario set up in advance. It exists, just as eternity itself, simultaneously with each moment of time. It is in the eternal presence of time to eternity, in an embrace, by the eternal moment, of a history in the process of its realization, perpetually fresh with newness or even (when free acts are involved) of unpredictability, that this plan is immutably fixed in heaven from all eternity."[23]

"When free beings are involved," writes Maritain, "one must say that . . . somehow [they] have their part to play—not by virtue of their power to act, in which [they] receive everything from God, but through the power to 'annihilate' or produce nothingness, in which they are primary causes—in the actual establishment of the eternal plan: in organizing this plan, God takes into account their initiatives of nothingness."[24]

Everything is possible amid the interplay of liberties and the repercussions on each other of our deeds, both good and bad. The secret of this permanent improvisation constituted by the innocent God's economy of grace has a name: the communion of saints. "We must therefore conclude," writes Journet, "that the outpouring of prevenient grace, be it 'regular' or 'miraculous,' the advancement of the City of God, and the progress made in the conversion of the world, will all be decided in large measure by the degree of fervent supplication offered by the friends of God."[25]

CHAPTER TWELVE

How Does God Know the Evil of Which He Has No Idea?

In publishing several years ago the first edition of this book whose title is *God without the Idea of Evil*,[1] I never dreamed that I would draw upon myself, alongside the heartfelt gratitude of many believers, the disapproval of certain theologians. Because this is a book of spirituality, I had not deemed it necessary to expose the theological justifications that could serve as a basis for the faithful when contemplating God's innocence in the face of the mystery of evil. A few months after my book was published, on the eve of the centenary of the birth of Maritain, during a conference in Paris at the Notre Dame Cathedral, I did at least take the opportunity to reveal as an expression of gratitude how much my spiritual approach was indebted to the mystical intuitions of Raïssa and to the metaphysical developments of Jacques.[2] Indeed, as their friend and disciple Cardinal Charles Journet wrote, we must simultaneously "learn to despise the absurd and worship the mystery."[3] Going back to the subject to examine how God knows evil, I would like to show more fully all that I owe to these three great contemporary witnesses of the innocence of God.

The title of the book, *God without the Idea of Evil*, is in fact only the repetition of a phrase of Saint Thomas Aquinas in the *Summa Theologiae* (I, q. 15, a. 3, ad. 1), quoted as an epigraph. Starting with the introduction, I suggested the way in which this leitmotif of my book ought to be understood, by insisting that *God does not conceive evil*. The divine ideas are the multiple ways in which creatures can participate in being. In God, who is Goodness itself, there are only ideas of creatures as they are: either as they are good or as their goodness suffers the deprivation of a property that they ought to have or that is due to them, such as blindness for a being whose nature normally possesses the sense of sight. Theologians call this second case a physical evil or an evil of nature.

How does God know physical evil, the deprivation among creatures of that which is their due? Charles Journet tells us that "it is in the good that these things ought to have but which they lack, that God knows this evil; but in him there are no ideas of evil."[4] And he quotes Saint Thomas himself: "Evil as such is nothingness, since it is a deprivation, for example blindness. Consequently, there really is in God an idea of the thing that is bad, indeed not insomuch as it is bad, but as a thing; and evil itself is known by God through the good opposed to that evil and which is lacking in the thing that is bad" (I Sent. dist. 36, q. 2, a. 3, ad. 1um).

In the domain of nature, because of the contingency of forms in a universe that is subject to change and is in the process of *becoming* (the "tohu-bohu" mentioned in Gen. 1:2), the good aimed at by the Creator inseparably involves an aspect of nothingness and deprivation. In this case "evil appears simply as the reverse side of the cosmic order."[5] These types of physical evil are therefore willed indirectly by the Creator to the extent that they accompany the forms that are directly willed by him. "They are therefore included in the divine ideas of good and measured by it."[6]

The error of the various theodicies that, like that of Leibniz, claim to account for all the evil that one finds in the world is to extend this form of knowledge—the willing of physical evils that is included in the divine ideas—to evil as such, that is, to the moral evil of sin and to its consequences for the human person: death (temporal and eternal) and the entire cortege of penalties that result from original sin (see Gen. 3:19, 22; Wis. 1:13–16 and 2:23–24; Rom. 5:12, etc.).

"And so then," writes Maritain,

> this philosopher tells us that it is good that a mother mourn the death of her child, because the machine of the world requires such pain in order to be more perfect. *Rachel is weeping for her sons and does not want to be comforted* (Matt. 2:18). If you were to try to explain this Leibnizian position to the mother in question, saying to her that this thing was necessary so that all the degrees of being could be filled, she would reply that she couldn't care less about the machine of the world; and that she wants her child back! And she would be right; because these matters are not solved by referring to the machine of the world but only in the night of faith, and through the cross of Jesus.[7]

"Undoubtedly," says Journet, "things like these arise from a nature made of spirit and of flesh; God, however, in his infinite goodness, had planned for man a condition of pure bliss. It was after the initial fault that pain and death entered our humanity. Rachel's cry is like a postulation of the earthly paradise; her refusal to be consoled, is like an obscure presentiment of what our first condition was."[8]

It is here that the words of Saint Thomas take on their full meaning: God has no idea of evil. Maritain writes:

> It is He *who invented Behemoth and Leviathan* and all the terrifying forms that inhabit the world of nature and life, predatory fish, devastating insects. It is *not* He who had the idea of all the filth and abominations, the contempt that is thrown into his own Face, the betrayals, the lust, the cowardice, the bestial wickedness, all the refined permissions [of evil], all the depravity of mind that it is given to his creatures to behold. All this is born only of the "annihilating" power of human liberty. It is from this abyss that it emerges. He [God] allows it as a creation of our power to produce nothingness.[9]

But if God permits moral evil, the source of all the misfortunes of fallen humanity, does he already know it by permitting it in advance, the way he knows the physical evils of the cosmos by wanting them indirectly in his creative ideas? Some scholastic theologians have not hesitated to account for moral evil by claiming that God knows sin in an "antecedent permissive decree" by which he permits it.[10] According to this theodicy, it is through "antecedent permissive decrees that God knows the sin of his creature because—oh yes, it's purely negative, he is careful not to cause anything!—he himself decided *not to cause* the good which is contrary to sin, in other words, because he himself decided *not to do* that without which the sin in question would most certainly take place."[11]

It is not at all surprising that the approach to God's innocence that I have attempted to trace in this book has attracted the disapproval of the proponents of this theodicy. They claim to defend the omnipotence of God as if it were an absolute power and not a power ordered to the design that he conceived to create and adopt through grace, men who are free and therefore capable of contradicting the divine love that goes out to them. These theologians also reason as if the capacity to conceive moral evil was a perfection and that therefore it should not be "missing" in God. This theodicy claims to defend the omnipotence of God in a rationalistic way that is in fact blasphemous with regard to divine innocence because, as Thomas recalls, "He cannot be directly the cause of sin. In like manner neither can he cause sin indirectly" (*Summa Theologiae* I-II, q. 79, a. 1) and "the first cause of the defect of grace is on our part" (q. 112, a. 3, ad. 2um). Even in the purely negative form of a permissive decree, antecedent in relation to our freely chosen sinful act, God cannot be indirectly the primary cause of our lack of grace. If things were otherwise, we would be confronted with a metaphysically refined form of the "withdrawal of grace," an idea cherished by the Jansenists. But Paul affirms that "the gifts . . . of God are irrevocable" (Rom. 11:29) and that "if we are faithless, he remains faithful—for he cannot deny himself" (2 Tim. 2:13).

If God does not know moral evil in the same way as physical evil, by conceiving in advance his permission, how then does he know it? Maritain approached this mystery in progressive stages. He first showed that moral evil can only be known by God in the act itself of the liberty of the person who sins: "This moment itself, when the creature takes the initiative of nothingness, thus demanding the permission to do evil, *precedes the permission* that is granted—God's non-will to remedy this initiative of nothingness—and is therefore not known in this permission; it can only be known in the actively deficient or annihilating free will."[12]

Later on Jacques Maritain went further by showing that God does not first know the moral evil as a deprivation of our free and fallible act in the way that he knows the possible deprivations of physical evil, deficiencies that are included in advance in his creative ideas: "Indeed, even before depriving humanity of its innocence and integrity, the sin of man who was created by God in a state of grace, 'deprives' the divine will of something it really wanted. . . . In his antecedent will, God wants all men to be saved, and he also wants all my acts to be good. If I sin, something that God wanted and loved will not be eternally. This is the result of my primary initiative."[13] As Thomas says, "Those who are not with God are, to the extent that He is in them, against God (cf. Matt. 12:30), *because they contradict the antecedent divine will*" (I Sent. dist. 47, q. 1, a. 2, ad. 1um; original emphasis).

If the antecedent will, by which God "desires everyone to be saved" (1 Tim. 2:4), cannot involve any antecedent permissive decrees conceiving moral evil but is instead directly "contradicted or thwarted" by sin, this is because this antecedent will is a kindhearted design of love to which God has actively committed himself. Indeed "this (antecedent) will is something real, even though it is conditional; it is not a simple wish or a vague indication of something that one does not positively *want*, but that one *would only like to be.*"[14]

God, of course, knows all the things that he has created according to the modality of their being. Therefore, "he perceives the liberty of created beings in the actual exercise of their free will. We know the act of free will is absolutely unpredictable. The divine science of vision perceives it eternally at the very instant when it is produced, in its very condition of being present."[15] Good acts of our liberty are conceived by God's grace, which enables us to produce them: "For we are what he has made us, created in Christ Jesus for good works, which God prepared beforehand to be our way of life" (Eph. 2:10); "it is God who is at work in you, enabling you both to will and to work for his good pleasure" (Phil. 2:13).

But the sin of our liberty, evil in the proper sense of the term, is inconceivable for God. In fact at the root of the evil act there is a contradiction of the benevolent will of God, a complete disdaining of the love that he is, a refusal to consider him the standard of our ultimate good, a hardening of heart with regard to the motion of his grace. It is therefore not enough to say that God knows moral evil in the sinful act of a person's liberty. In the last years of his life, Jacques Maritain tried to express the ultimate mystery of God's "knowledge" of evil: God perceives our sin, and in this sense only he "knows" that which remains inconceivable for him in a redemptive acceptance of the unacceptable. The rejection of divine love that lies at the base of all sin constitutes for God, in the words of Jacques Maritain, "the *inadmissible that needs to be accepted*. By respecting with absolute magnanimity the free will of his creatures and their initiatives of nothingness, by allowing sin in view of a higher good by which He will super-abundantly compensate it, God consents to that which is '*inadmissible* to God,' not in order to be subjected to it (how could he ever be subjected to anything?), but in order to seize it victoriously."[16]

God only perceives the sinful free act whereby we elude his grace and contradict his antecedent will by taking hold of it in an extra, superabundant redemptive love. "Before triumphing over this 'unacceptable thing' by a greater good that will compensate for it super-abundantly later on, He Himself, far from submitting to it, elevates it above everything by consenting to it: by accepting such a deprivation (which does not affect His being, but only the relationship of the creature to Him), he takes hold of it and carries it like a trophy, attesting to the divinely pure grandeur of the victorious Acceptance."[17]

God conceives the evil of sin, neither directly nor indirectly in his creative ideas, nor in any so-called antecedent permissive decree. He can only perceive this inconceivable and unacceptable rejection of the love that he himself is (1 John 4:16) in a redemptive acceptance whose supreme expression is the mystery of Jesus. Moral evil is the "contradiction of sinners" that Jesus endured (Heb. 12:3), because as Maritain says in a passage quoted earlier, "the eternal splendor of the victorious Acceptance (we have no proper way of naming it) [has made itself known to us] in the image par excellence, the image of flesh and blood of the Son of God suffering death."[18] This redemptive acceptance of evil by God exposes in advance the character at once ridiculous and blasphemous of any attempt to account for the evil of sin in a speculative theodicy.

NOTES

Translator's Preface

1. J.-M. Garrigues, *Par des sentiers resserrés: Itinéraire d'un religieux en des temps incertains* (Paris: Presses de la Renaissance, 2007).
2. J.-M. Garrigues, *A l'heure de notre mort: accueillir la vie éternelle* (Paris: de l'Emmanuel, 2001).
3. J.-M. Garrigues, *L'Esprit qui dit: "Père!" et le problème du Filoque*, préface du P. Louis Bouyer de l'Oratoire, coll. "Croire et savoir" (Paris: Téqui, 1981).
4. J.-M. Garrigues, *Dieu sans idée du mal: La liberté de l'homme au cœur de Dieu* (Paris: Critérion, 1982; réed. Paris: Desclée, 1990, Édition Ad Solem, 2016).
5. J.-M. Garrigues, dir., *L'unique Israël de Dieu: Approches chrétiennes du mystère d'Israël* (Paris: Critérion, 1987).
6. J.-M. Garrigues, *Le dessein de Dieu à travers ses alliances: Catéchèses pour adultes* (Paris: de l'Emmanuel, 2003).
7. See the acts of the seminar at the University of Tel Aviv in 1995, published in *Philosophia: Philosophical Quarterly of Israel* 30, nos. 1–4 (March 2003).
8. J.-M. Garrigues, "Anti-judaïsme et théologie d'Israël" [Anti-Judaism and the theology of Israel], in *Radici dell'antijudaismo in ambiente cristiano: Atti del Simposio teologico-storico, Città del Vaticano dal 30 ottobre al 1 novembre 1997*, coll. "Atti e documenti," no. 8 (Vatican City: Libreria editrice vaticana, 2000); and J.-M. Garrigues, "L'Eglise pénitente pour le consentement donné par ses enfants à l'intolérance et à la violence religieuse" [Repentance of the church for those of her children who consented to intolerance and religious violence], in *L'Inquisizione: Atti del Simposio internazionale, Città del Vaticano, 29–31 ottobre 1998*, coll. "Studi e testi," no. 417 (Vatican City: Biblioteca apostolica vaticana, 2003).
9. The original Italian version of this article was published in *La Civiltà Cattolica* 2, no. 3959 (June 13, 2015): 493–510.

10. Antonio Spadaro, S.J., "A Church of the Pure or a Mixed Fish Net? An Interview with Jean-Miguel Garrigues, O.P.," *America*, June 19, 2015.

11. J.-M. Garrigues in collaboration with Alain Thomasset, S.J., *Une morale souple mais non sans boussole: Répondre aux doutes des cardinaux sur "Amoris laetitia"* (Paris: du Cerf, 2017).

Chapter One. The Omnipotence of the Father

1. *Translator's Note*: At the same time, man was meant to receive creation from the hands of God not as a master who exploits it arbitrarily but as a cultivator, caretaker, and developer who looks after it with love, and above all as a priest who returns it to God with thanksgiving. At the Resurrection, the manifestation of the glory of the children of God will bring about the transformation (in ways that are impossible for us to imagine now) of the entire material creation, including, one might think, nonhuman life.

2. *Translator's Note*: In the Old Testament, the various covenants—with Adam and all humanity at creation, with the nations represented by Noah and his descendants, with Abraham and the patriarchs concerning the Promise, and with Moses and the nation of Israel at the time of the liberation from Egypt and passage into the Promised Land—were all preparations for the coming of Christ, and his grace of redemption is already prefigured and at work in them. God never abolished these covenants, and those who strive to observe them with faith are implicitly sanctified and justified in advance through Jesus Christ. This is especially true of the Jews, including those alive after the coming of Jesus and who observe faithfully and in good conscience the Old Testament law, awaiting with us the full realization of God's design of salvation. Jean-Miguel Garrigues has treated this question at great length in *Le dessein de Dieu à travers ses alliances: Catéchèses pour adultes* [The design of God seen through his covenants: A catechism for adults] (Paris: de l'Emmanuel, 2003); and, for all that concerns the Jewish people, in *Le Peuple de la Première Alliance: Approches chrétiennes du mystère d'Israël* [The People of the Old Covenant: A Christian approach to the mystery of Israel], coll. "Théologies" (Paris: du Cerf, 2011). Unfortunately, these works have not yet been translated into English.

Chapter Three. The Innocence of the Father in Our Adoption

1. *Translator's Note*: The phrase "kindhearted design" reproduces the way in which Garrigues renders a particular Greek word that designates God's goodwill toward us. The expression constitutes the central notion on which the theology of this book is based. Garrigues justifies and explains this translation further in

chapter 6. The NRSV translates the verse as "according to the *good pleasure* of his will"; the New Jerusalem Bible, as "Such was his purpose and *good pleasure*."

2. *Translator's Note*: Once again italicized words represent Garrigues's rendering of the Greek. The NRSV has "according to the good pleasure of his will."

3. *Translator's Note*: These expressions reproduce Garrigues's very literal renditions of the Greek. The NRSV translates, "to make everyone see what is *the plan of the mystery*. The New Jerusalem Bible has "throwing light on the *inner workings of the mystery*."

4. *Translator's Note*: The italicized words reproduce Garrigues's rendition of the Greek, which also corresponds to the French edition of the Jerusalem Bible. The NRSV has "according to his *good pleasure* that he set forth in Christ." The New Jerusalem Bible has "according to the *good pleasure* which he determined beforehand in Christ."

Chapter Four. The Glorious Growth of the Liberty of the Sons of God

1. *Translator's Note*: See chap. 3, n. 4.

2. *Translator's Note*: Once again this is Garrigues's literal rendition of the Greek. The NRSV has "as a plan for the fullness of time." See also chap. 3, n. 3.

3. *Translator's Note*: Garrigues's rendition of the Greek. The NRSV has "to gather up all things in him, things in heaven and things on earth." The New Jerusalem Bible has "that he would bring everything together under Christ, as head, everything in the heavens and everything on earth."

4. *Translator's Note*: During the glorious liturgy of the Easter Vigil, the church, with immense gratitude and love, is contemplating precisely and above all the *means* of her redemption in the person of the crucified and risen Lord Jesus. She sees in him the eloquent expression of love unto folly for humanity. Totally enthralled, she responds in the folly of love, saying, "O felix culpa—o happy fault," knowing that without the fault of original sin, she would not have contemplated her beloved redeemer in quite the same way. The "felix culpa" should be taken for what it in fact is: not a foundation on which to build a speculative theology, but instead a sublimely poetic expression of love.

5. *Translator's Note*: The NRSV has "Glory to God in the highest heaven, and on earth peace among those whom he favors."

6. *Translator's Note*: The NRSV has "This is my Son, my Beloved, with whom I am well pleased."

7. *Translator's Note*: Elsewhere Garrigues writes on this same topic. If Adam and Eve had not sinned, "they would have known a passage from the life of history, from the temporal life, to the eternal life. It would still have been a 'death' in the sense that there would have been a transition from one state to another,

something like what faith tells us occurred in what is referred to as the 'dormition' of the Virgin Mary at the end of her earthly existence. But even this analogy is only a very distant one, because the Blessed Virgin, in her association with the Redemption of her son, shared at the same time many aspects of fallen humanity: hence she too endured suffering. So it is not really possible to affirm that the form of 'death' that she knew was what our first parents and all humanity would have known if they had not sinned but followed the ways of God. For an innocent humanity this 'death' would not have been linked to the trials and sufferings of Christ's Redemption and Paschal mystery, as was the case for Mary, but instead it would have been a passage from the love of that which is limited to that which is unlimited, from the temporal to the eternal, a transition, an ecstasy, an exit from the limits of a history which evolves and changes constantly, into the eternal present moment of God." J.-M. Garrigues, *A l'heure de notre mort* [At the hour of our death] (Paris: Éditions de l'Emmanuel, 2000). An English-language edition of this book is currently in preparation.

Chapter Seven. The Son as the Lamb Who Was Slain from the Beginning of the World

1. *Translator's Note*: This word order is proposed as a variant by the NRSV.
2. *Translator's Note*: The NRSV gives this word order in the text itself.

Chapter Eleven. God without the Idea of Evil

1. Raïssa Maritain, *Journal de Raïssa, Published by Jacques Maritain* (Paris: Desclée de Brouwer, 1963), 210.
2. Isidore Ducasse, "Préface à des poèmes futurs," dans *Œuvres complètes* du Comte de Lautréamont (Paris: GLM, 1938).
3. Jacques Maritain, *Approches sans entraves* (Paris: Fayard, 1973), 315; original emphasis.
4. Jacques Maritain, *De Bergson à Thomas d'Aquin* (New York: Editions de la Maison Française, 1944), 229; original emphasis.
5. Charles Journet, Jacques Maritain, and Philippe de la Trinité, *Le péché de l'ange* (Paris: Beauchesne, 1961), 55–56; original emphasis.
6. Charles Journet, *L'Église du Verbe Incarné* (Paris: Desclée de Brouwer, 1969), 3:172, 280–81; original emphasis.
7. Maritain, *De Bergson*, 229; translator's emphasis.

8. Jacques Maritain, "La clef des chants," *Frontières de la poésie et autres essais* (Paris: Rouart, 1935), 187–88 n. 1.
9. Journet, *L'Église*, 222; translator's emphasis.
10. Jacques Maritain, *Neuf Leçons sur les notions premières de la philosophie morale* (Paris: Téqui, 1951), 175–76.
11. Maritain, *Journal de Raïssa*, 289.
12. Ibid., 77; original emphasis.
13. Maritain, *Approches sans entraves*, 312.
14. Maritain, *Journal de Raïssa*, 55.
15. Ibid., 221.
16. Ibid., 365–70; original emphasis.
17. Charles Journet, *Entretiens sur la grâce* (Paris: Desclée de Brouwer, 1961), 102–3.
18. Maritain, *Journal de Raïssa*, 369.
19. Maritain, *Neuf Leçons*, 189–90.
20. Journet, *L'Église*, 218; original emphasis.
21. Maritain, *Neuf Leçons*, 190.
22. Jacques Maritain, *Dieu et la permission du mal* (Paris: Desclée de Brouwer, 1963), 85.
23. Journet, *L'Eglise*, 167 n.
24. Jacques Maritain, *Court traité de l'existence et de l'existant* (Paris: Hartmann, 1947), 183–84.
25. Charles Journet, *Le mal* (Paris: Desclée de Brouwer, 1961), 187.

Chapter Twelve. How Does God Know the Evil of Which He Has No Idea?

1. Garrigues, *Dieu sans idée du mal*.
2. The lecture has become chapter 11 of this book.
3. Charles Journet, *Le mal, essai théologique* (Paris: Desclée de Brouwer, 1961), dedication.
4. Ibid., 196.
5. Journet, *L'Église*, 3:172.
6. Journet, *Le mal*, 226.
7. Maritain, *De Bergson*, 223–26; translator's emphasis.
8. Journet, *Le mal*, 226.
9. In Maritain, *Court traité*, 191–92; translator's emphasis.
10. Cf. Maritain's rebuttal of this position in *Dieu et la permission du mal*, 20–25.

11. Ibid., 70; original emphasis.
12. Maritain, *Court traité*, 177; original emphasis.
13. Maritain, *Neuf Leçons*, 175–76.
14. Maritain, *Dieu et la permission du mal*, 98; original emphasis. See also on this point Jean-Pierre Arfeuil, "Le dessein sauveur de Dieu et la doctrine de la prédestination chez S. Thomas d'Aquin," *Revue Thomiste* 4 (1974): 607–8.
15. Maritain, *Court traité*, 174–75.
16. Maritain, *Approches sans entraves*, 308; original emphasis.
17. Ibid., 309.
18. Ibid., 312.

INDEX

agape, 10, 25
Amoris laetitia, xviii
Annunciation, the, 73
Assumption of Moses (apocryphal writing), 118
Augustine, Saint, 110
  Confessions, 152

Baruch, book of, 82
Bouyer, Louis, xiii–xiv
Bread of Life (discourse), 107–8, 131

Carthusian order, xxvi
Catechism of the Catholic Church, xv, xvii
Catherine of Siena, Saint, xi, 44–45, 100–101, 103, 133–37, 142–43
  the *Dialogue*, 135
  intercessory prayers of, 140–41
Colossians, Epistle to the, 58
Corinthians, First Epistle to the, 28, 108, 121
Corinthians, Second Epistle to the, 34
Cottier, Georges, O.P., xvii
Council of Trent, 159

Daniel, book of, 85, 118
deification, 56, 58, 66, 68, 90, 158–59
deifying grace, 35, 57, 63
Descartes, René, 33
Deuteronomy, book of, 105
divine omnipotence, 20–21
divinization, 57–58
Dominic, Saint, xxiii, xxvi, 133
  night prayer of, 141–43
dormition, 66, 73

Eastern liturgy, 54
Ecclesiastes, book of, 23, 28
Ephesians, Epistle to the, 19, 46–48, 55, 59, 64, 77
Eucharistic Prayer IV, 156
Exodus, book of, 71, 80–81
Exsultet, 59
Ezekiel, book of, 82–84

filioque, xiv
forgiveness, 53–54, 80–81
Fra Angelico, ix
  The Mocking of Christ, ix, xxiii–xxvi, 52, 104, 115
Francis, Pope, xviii

Genesis, book of, 7, 9, 24, 35, 150
   conception of human liberty in, 13–16
   creation story in, 11–12, 62–63
   —Trinitarian implications of, 42–43, 57
   drunkenness of Noah in, 122
   man as heir of creation in, 32
Good Friday, 70, 115–16
Gregory of Nyssa, Saint, 156

Habakkuk, book of, 122
Hebrews, Epistle to the, 10, 32, 39, 115, 126
Holy Thursday, 105–6
Hosea, book of, 86, 127

Incarnation, xxvi, 27, 35, 63, 66, 84, 95, 99, 105
   redemptive nature of, 58–60, 63, 76, 95
   relationship to iconography, xxi
Institut Catholique (Paris), xiv
Irenaeus of Lyons, Saint, 9, 15–16
Isaiah, book of, 38, 40, 83, 85–86, 128, 142

Jansenists, 167
Jeremiah, book of, 124–25
Job, book of, 117, 138
John, gospel of, 29, 32, 39, 75, 106–8, 110
John Paul II, xv, xvii
Journet, Charles, xii, 153–55, 160–66
Jude, Epistle of, 118
justice, 8, 16, 76, 138

kingdom of God, 27, 39
Kinzer, Mark, xv–xvi

Lamentations, book of, 123
last judgment, the, 139
Last Supper, the, 105, 107–9, 111, 113–14, 120–21, 130
Lautréamont, 148–49
Leibniz, Gottfried Wilhelm, 165
Levites, 70, 120
Luke, gospel of, 104–5, 113, 115
   Last Supper narrative in, 120
Lustiger, Jean-Marie, xvi–xvii

Manichean dualism, 150
Maritain, Jacques, xii–xiii, 147, 149, 153–54, 161–62, 164, 166–68
   on God's "knowledge" of evil, 169
   on human fallibility, 151
   on image of crucified Jesus, 158
   on sin as offense against God, 157
Maritain, Raïssa, 147, 164
   diary of, 148
   on image of crucified Jesus, 157
   on self-sacrifice, 158–59
Masaccio, 61
Matthew, gospel of, 38, 77, 99
Maximus the Confessor, Saint, 57, 156
Mystical Body of Christ, 61–62, 137

Nostra aetate, xvii

Origen, 156
original sin, 13, 35–36, 39, 49, 60, 63, 66, 68, 89, 152

Pascal, Blaise, xxv, 103, 134
Passion, the (event), 71, 113, 130, 135–36
Passover, 31–32, 70–71
Pentecost, 73, 124

Peter, First Epistle of, 67, 70, 86, 99
Peter, Second Epistle of, 65
Philippians, Epistle to the, 37–38
Pontifical Academy of Theology (Rome), xviii
predestination, 35, 46–47, 75, 134
prevenient grace, 73, 156, 160–61
prodigal son, 6, 13, 15, 36–37, 81, 87, 96–97, 139
Proverbs, book of, 29

Ratzinger, Joseph, xv
Raymond of Capua, 133
Redemption, the (event), 56, 59–61, 64, 76–77, 106, 132, 136
Revelation, book of, 8, 23, 33, 89, 94–95, 128–29
Rimbaud, Arthur, 22
Romans, Epistle to the, 9, 57
Rublev, Andrei, ix
   Icon of the Hospitality of Abraham (Icon of the Trinity), ix, xi, xxi–xxiii, xxii (fig. 1), xxvii, 29, 79, 102

Saint Nizier (Lyons), xviii
San Marco Convent (Florence), xxiii, xxvi
Saulchoir (Dominican school), xv
Shroud of Turin, xxiv
Silouan of Mount Athos, 61
Simeon the New Theologian, Saint, 88
Solesmes, xviii

Song of Solomon, 86
sons of Zebedee, 130
Spadaro, Antonio, S.J., xviii–xix
Suffering Servant, the, 71, 79, 99

tetragrammaton, 80
theodicy, ix, 167, 169
Thomas Aquinas, Saint, ix–xi, xiii, xxvi, 48, 148, 154, 160
   Commentary on the Sentences, 165, 168
   Media vita, 54, 81
   Summa Theologiae, 147, 165, 167
Thomas Aquinas Institute, xviii
Thomasset, Alain, xviii
Timothy, Second Epistle to, 28
tohu-bohu, concept of, 7, 150, 165
transfiguration, 64–65
Trinity, 25, 28, 31, 54, 62, 93
   as dialogue of creation, 25, 33–36, 42–43, 79
   humanity's entry into, 47, 56–59
   and Rublev's icon, xxi, xxiii

Verne, Jules, 8
Vigny, Alfred de, 6

Wisdom, book of, 30, 53, 118
World Council of Churches, xiii

Yom Kippur, 80, 118

Zechariah, book of, 71, 85–86, 117–18

JEAN-MIGUEL GARRIGUES, O.P.
is professor emeritus at Domuni Universitas in Toulouse
and a member of the Pontifical Academy of Theology.

GREGORY CASPRINI, O.S.B.
has translated numerous works from French into English,
including Dom Eugène Cardine's *An Overview of Gregorian Chant* and
Dom Jacques Hourlier's *Reflections on the Spirituality of Gregorian Chant*.

www.ingramcontent.com/pod-product-compliance
Lightning Source LLC
Chambersburg PA
CBHW070358100426
42812CB00005B/1551